Si tu veux vraiment

connaître la montagne,

lorsque tu seras arrivé en haut,

continue de grimper.

Chamonix mountain guide, 1954

(If you really want

to know the mountain,

when you get to the top,

keep climbing.)

Vail

Triumph of a Dream

By Peter W. Seibert

With William Oscar Johnson

Vail: Triumph of a Dream

Published by
Mountain Sports Press
929 Pearl Street, Suite 200
Boulder, Colorado 80302
In conjunction with
Vail Resorts Management Company

Editor-in-Chief: Bill Grout
Associate Publisher: Alan Stark
Art Director: Michelle Klammer Schrantz
Associate Art Director: Scott Kronberg
Managing Editor: Chris Salt
Sales Representative: Andy Hawk

ISBN 0-9717748-5-4
Library of Congress Cataloging-in
Publication Data applied for.

Distributed to the Book Trade by
PUBLISHERS GROUP WEST

First Paperback Edition, October 2002

Printed in Canada
by Friesens Corp.

A SUBSIDIARY OF:

TIME4MEDIA

929 Pearl St., Suite 200
Boulder, CO 80302
303-448-7617

CONTENTS

FOREWORD
BY JEAN-CLAUDE KILLY

Killy got a lot of congratulatory kisses in the Sixties.

When I was racing in the 1960s, I loved going to Vail. The races were usually in the springtime, the weather was warm, the sun often shining, and the courses always in great shape. At Vail I didn't have to be so serious. I could clown around a little bit, wear a Vail baseball cap turned around backward or a bright pink shirt with my striped racing pants. Ski racing was fun. I remember in March 1967 I won four consecutive races at Vail—a slalom on Thursday, a giant slalom on Friday, a downhill on Saturday, and another giant slalom on Sunday.

I also liked Vail because the people were so friendly. In Europe I sometimes couldn't even leave my hotel room without being mobbed by fans, but at Vail I could go out at night, go dancing with my friends, wear a cowboy hat, barbecue some good American steaks, play poker, just relax. The people respected my privacy and yet they were always smiling and friendly and ready to have a good time. That was wonderful, especially in March when I was tired from the long racing season.

I returned to Vail many times after that, to race on the pro circuit, to compete in fund-raising events for my friend Jimmie Heuga's MS foundation, or just to ski the powder in the Back Bowls. Sometimes I would ski with Pete Seibert, Vail's founder and a former ski racer himself. I could see that Pete was very proud of Vail, as he had good reason to be. A world-class ski resort had grown up on this mountain that Pete had discovered. But in those days I didn't know the whole story: how Pete had had a dream of building his own ski resort since he was a boy; how he nearly died fighting with the famous 10th Mountain Division during World War II; how he spent ten years searching the Colorado Rockies for a mountain to build his own ski resort; and how, with the help of many others, he made his dream come true at Vail.

This book tells the whole incredible story. Enjoy.

Those who dream by night

in the dusty recesses of their minds

wake in the morning

to find that all was vanity;

but the dreamers of the day

are dangerous...for they

may act on their dream...

and make it possible.

T.E. Lawrence, *Seven Pillars of Wisdom*

Vail Village, mid 1960s

Above Mid Vail, early 1960s

Wine and song, early 1970s

Pete Seibert, 1961

Golf before the golf course was built, mid 1960s

U.S. Ski Team, 1964

Roger Staub on Tourist Trap, late 1960s

Ski School Director Morrie Shepard, 1963

Photo shoot, mid 1960s

Vail Valley, 1960

Instruction clinic, 1963

Pro racer Tyler Palmer, early 1970s

UP THE NO-NAME MOUNTAIN

It was an hour before morning light on Tuesday, March 19, 1957, when Earl Eaton and I parked my army-surplus Jeep on the snowy shoulder of U.S. Highway 6 and prepared to climb a mountain that had no name.

The stars were out, and it promised to be a clear and sunny day—just as we had hoped. We laced up our leather ski boots and strapped climbing skins onto our 215-centimeter Head skis. We stepped into bear-trap bindings and lashed long

Pete Seibert atop Vail Mountain, 1958

leather thongs around our ankles to prevent losing a ski in bottomless powder. We then put on our packs, which contained our lunches, first-aid kits, dry socks, and other paraphernalia necessary for an all-day marathon. Finally, we poked our shoulder-high ski poles into the snow, turned south, and began the ascent in knee-deep powder.

It was tough going from the start, deep and steep, and we often traded places for breaking trail. After a half mile or so, we were panting and perspiring.

"God, I hope this is worth the trip," I said to Earl.

He pondered this question as we continued to climb. "It looked like a damn good ski mountain when I saw it before," he finally said.

"You saw it in the summertime," I chided him. "You couldn't

judge snow conditions or wind conditions. I hope we're not wasting our time."

He shrugged. "Hunting for a good ski mountain is never a waste of time." He plunged ahead into the powder.

* * * * *

Earl Eaton was thirty-five years old, a native of Edwards, just fifteen miles away down Route 6. Born Westerner though he was, Earl seemed to me more like the pragmatic, imperturbable New England Yankees I had grown up with in Massachusetts and New Hampshire. He spoke directly but softly, if at all, and usually his contribution to a discussion was brief, pointed, and firmly rooted in common sense.

He was also a powerful skier who worked as a snowcat driver and ski patrolman in the winter. In summer he transformed himself into a uranium prospector, traveling tirelessly through Colorado mountain country with his Geiger counter. His search for minerals had given him a unique familiarity with vast areas of isolated Colorado mountain terrain, much of it rarely visited by other human beings. But uranium wasn't the only treasure Earl Eaton was prospecting for. He was also looking for a mountain that might someday be turned into a splendid new ski area, a mountain with vast rolling slopes—some steep, some gentle, some wooded, some wide open—all running down three or four beautifully falling miles to the base from a suitably snowy summit.

Earl and I had shared this desire to find the perfect ski

Earl Eaton, 1959

Unchanging parorama: the view of the Gore Range from Vail Mountain as it looked to Pete and Earl on March 19, 1957.

mountain since we first met in Aspen in 1947. During the intervening ten years, we had explored a dozen or more sites, including the Collegiate Peaks west of Salida, Monarch Pass, and the San Juan range in southwest Colorado, as well as a hill or two in the Eagle Valley. We had come away convinced that none were up to the standards of the mountain we wanted. But we were never discouraged.

* * * * *

Both of us had spent the winter of 1957 working at the Loveland Pass ski area. I was the area manager; Earl was a mountain maintenance man and ski patroller. During the days we worked to serve the trickle of skiers (only one hundred to two hundred on weekdays, perhaps a thousand on weekends) who dared to drive the slick, twisting fifty miles on U.S. 6 from Denver to Loveland. Nights we spun dreams around a potbelly

stove in Buckley's Store, down the road in Silver Plume. Always the talk was of skiing: how to do it, where to do it, how to build a money-making ski resort. At the time, there were only a handful of functioning ski areas in Colorado, including Aspen, Winter Park, Loveland, Arapahoe Basin, Howelson Hill in Steamboat Springs, and Berthoud Pass. But in those days every ski bum, every snowplow driver, every ski patrolman in Colorado firmly believed that if he could only find the right mountain with the right contours and the right weather patterns he could quit his job, raise some money, and build a ski resort that would make him rich and famous.

Of course, I was possessed by the same dream—only I had been hooked on it for a lot longer than most. My vision of finding and developing my own ski area first came to me when I was a little boy living in New England. In that part of the world, the mountains were smaller and the ski runs were shorter and generally covered with hard ice. But I didn't care. Any hill I could ski on became part of my imaginary resort.

One of the runs I liked most was my daily milk route, between my family's farmhouse and our neighbor's cow barn, a distance of maybe five hundred yards. Each afternoon I set off from my house carrying an empty one-quart milk bottle in each hand. I reached exciting downhill speeds as I descended to the barn and even managed to land a ten-foot ski jump near the bottom. Climbing back up was something else. Burdened now with bottles full of fresh, warm milk, I laboriously herringboned up. I tried to ignore the effort involved by imagining I had my own rope tow. I had heard that in Woodstock, Vermont, someone had opened a ski area with an uphill tow powered by a Model T Ford engine. He had invited the world to share this little mountain. That's what I wanted to do. And as I grew older, the dream only grew larger.

THE UTES

Long before there was a ski area, and long before there were white ranchers in the area, the valley near present-day Vail was home to small bands of Ute Indians, who used it as a hunting ground and summer residence. As the oldest continuous residents of Colorado, the Utes roamed the southern Rockies in small family units, hunting for deer, elk, and antelope; gathering seeds, wild berries, and fruits; and occasionally planting corn, beans, and squash in mountain meadows.

Their way of life changed drastically after the Spanish introduced horses to the Utes around 1630. Horses allowed them to hunt bison on Colorado's eastern plains and engage in horse racing and high-stakes gambling. They became skilled at stealing horses from other Native American tribes. Eventually overzealous U.S. government agents tried to wean the Utes off gambling and stealing by prodding them to settle down and raise pumpkins, using their horses for plowing. Tension over this issue led to the Meeker Massacre of 1879, in which eleven people were killed. After that, white settlers took over much of the Utes' land in western Colorado and herded many of them into arid eastern Utah. In 1950, the U.S. government finally made restitution to the Utes for stealing their land, awarding them $32 million, which, after attorneys' fees, became only $5.5 million.

In the late Fifties, John Hanson's ranch spanned both sides of U.S. 6 and Gore Creek, where Vail Village now stands.

* * * * *

In the winter of 1957, I was thirty-two. My life had already included more adventures than most men face in twice that many years. I had gone to war with the U.S. Army's famed 10th Mountain Division and suffered devastating wounds over much of my body. After a painful postwar recovery, I had left New England to find a mountain in the West where I could build ski lifts and a village at its base. I worked as a ski patroller in Aspen and made the 1950 U.S. Alpine Ski Team. Then I attended a French-language hotel school in Switzerland, where I learned from the Swiss the fine art of hospitality and service. In 1955 I had married Elizabeth "Betty" Pardee, and we now had a two-year-old son. I was managing my first ski area at Loveland while looking for one to build from scratch.

Then, early in the winter of 1957, Earl Eaton confided to me that he had seen this nameless mountain west of Vail Pass that was rarely visited, except by stray prospectors and shepherds. He had explored it thoroughly with his Geiger counter ticking. There was no uranium to be mined, but he told me that it was

the damnedest ski mountain he had ever seen. He said that the only reason someone hadn't already developed it was because no one could see the top slopes or the miraculous Back Bowls from the valley below.

* * * * *

Floundering upward in three feet of snow along a faintly visible logging road, it took us two hours to slog the first two miles. I thought of the old days in New Hampshire and the round-shouldered mountains there. Compared to those hills, this was like climbing the Himalaya. It occurred to me that I should be damned grateful I wasn't carrying any full bottles of milk or lugging my ninety-pound army rucksack on this strenuous trek.

We eventually reached the site of a ramshackle sawmill on Mill Creek. Then the logging road petered out as we turned west and entered a dense, silent forest of lodgepole pine and spruce. We climbed in soft, knee-deep powder, cutting back and forth through the woods along a narrow skid road once used by loggers. After almost

Above: In all of their previous explorations throughout Colorado, Pete and Earl had seen nothing to match the Back Bowls, an almost treeless universe of boundless powder, open slopes, and open sky. Below: Vail's deep, consistent snowfall, sheltered from the westerly winds, was one of the features that appealed to both Pete and Earl.

two hours in the trees, we broke out into sunny, open terrain and faced a vast landscape consisting only of sun-splashed snowy slopes, dotted here and there with perfectly sculptured spruce and fir trees, rolling up the hill almost as far as the eye could see.

I didn't know it then, of course, but this place would become Mid Vail, where the ski trails Swingsville, Zot, and Ramshorn would all come together from the summit; where skiers would drift off to the Cookshack restaurant for lunch or take the Number 4 lift back to the top for another run; or where they would head to the bottom of the ski area on

BLUE SKY BASIN

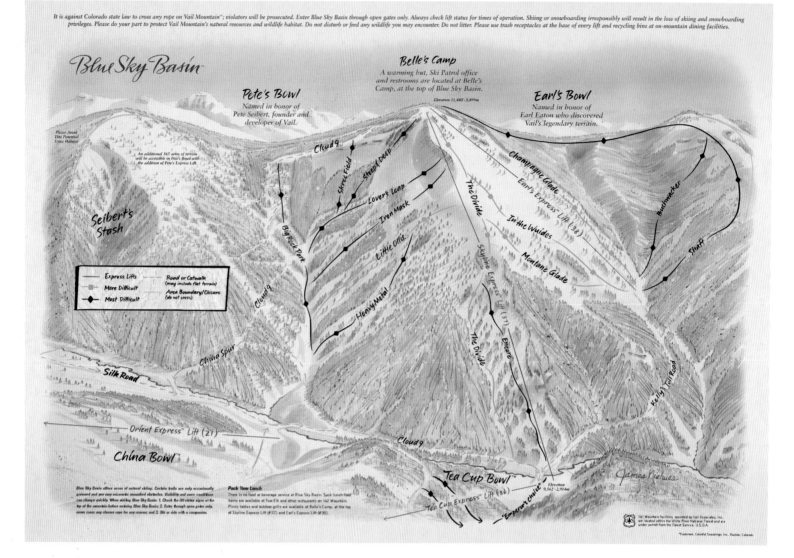

Blue Sky Basin

Belle's Camp
A warming hut, Ski Patrol office and restrooms are located at Belle's Camp, at the top of Blue Sky Basin.
Elevation 11,440'-3,494m

Pete's Bowl
Named in honor of Pete Seibert, founder and developer of Vail.

Earl's Bowl
Named in honor of Earl Eaton who discovered Vail's legendary terrain.

Not until the week following the dawn of the year 2000—almost forty-three years after Earl and I had made that initial climb—was the last big piece of Vail Mountain completed. The event brought fresh reminders of the intense blueprinting, planning, mapping, and modeling we had done to transform that precious terrain into a skiers' paradise.

The final element of the resort master plan called for a massive expansion into two large bowls that would add 19 percent more terrain to the Vail area, already the largest in the U.S. At first this section was simply called Two Elk, after the creek at the bottom of the drainage. Later the name was changed to an engineer's term, Category III, and finally the area was given a more poetic moniker: Blue Sky Basin. It formally opened on January 6, 2000—an unforgettable day for me.

The weather was identical to that on the day Earl Eaton and I had first climbed the mountain in 1957—sparkling sunshine on deep virgin powder. Beyond that, however, the scene couldn't have been more different. Earl and I were there, yes, but we were far from alone this time, and the mountain was far from silent. The place rang with speeches and cheers and noisy applause from a crowd of skiers and snowboarders in the thousands. There were TV crews, news anchors talking into microphones, reporters taking notes. The story made the evening news and turned up on the following day's front pages of more than a few Colorado papers. One headline told it all: PETE AND EARL'S DREAM COMES ALIVE.

The portion of Blue Sky Basin opened that day covered 520 acres and is known as Earl's Bowl. The second part of the expansion will open for the 2000-01 season and will be called Pete's Bowl.

Earl and I cut a blue ribbon, and I watched with joy and excitement as thousands of eager powderhounds charged down

Previous page: On the ridge between Pete's Bowl and Earl's Bowl, with the Sawatch Range in the background.

into the bottomless powder. Most of the snow was waist deep, yet in some places it rose over their heads. Yelps, yodels, and yips of pure joy echoed out of Blue Sky Basin. The noise grew fainter as the multitude descended.

As I watched people cut through the powder, the years rolled back and I thought of all the emotional peaks and valleys, the triumphs and the tragedies that had made up the fabric of my life at Vail.

* * * * *

I remember opening day in December 1962. We had no more than ankle-deep snow at the top, and the lower slopes were barren. Only a handful of people showed up, mostly local cowboys and their families who wanted to ride the lift for the view. It wasn't until six days later that the first real storm arrived. Actually, opening day wasn't even the worst day for business that first season. On January 10, 1963, we sold exactly twelve lift tickets, at five dollars apiece. But by the end of the season, we had sold a modestly successful fifty-five thousand lift tickets, many of them thanks to the genius of our marketing man, Bob Parker. (He would later produce the well-known "Ski the Rockies" campaign and shrewdly use World Cup races to make Vail a player on the international map of ski resorts.)

Vail never possessed the chic of Sun Valley or the glitz of Aspen, so we didn't attract the movie-star crowd or jet-setters. What we had, and what we wanted, were solid family skiers, and that became our image. Still, we could satisfy every kind of skier, from the Colorado weekend set to the wealthy foreign crowd, from daredevil double-diamond experts to happy children snowplowing down

beginners' trails.

In those early years, I treated our skiers almost as if they were visitors to my home. I used to post a list of guests' names each week in the lift crew's office so that they could call out, "Good morning, Mr. Jones! Good morning, Mrs. Smith!" as the skiers boarded the gondola for Mid Vail.

Vail reflected my values, my wishes, my dreams. It reflected my life. And because it was my life, it contained much pain along with much happiness, much good luck with much bad, much darkness along with much light.

Blue Sky Basin's northern exposure keeps the shadows long and the snow light and dry.

Why Vail?

It's called Vail because Vail was already the name of the nearby mountain pass on U.S. Highway 6 just to the east—and because I liked short names like Aspen and Alta. Not that there weren't other choices. One possibility might have been another single-word name—Gore—after the magnificent Gore Range to the northeast and Gore Creek Valley, which lay at the foot of the mountain. But Gore would have been an odd, even perverse choice. For one thing, the range's namesake, Sir St. George Gore, may never have set foot in this part of Colorado. Worse, he was a boorish rich man, a drunken Irish baronet and rapacious hunter who rampaged around the West for three years in the 1850s butchering elk, deer, and buffalo for trophies and leaving countless carcasses where they fell.

So Gore wouldn't do. But Vail? That would be Charles Vail, chief engineer of the Colorado highway department from 1930 until his death in 1945. To put it briefly, he spent his life spreading pavement over Colorado's virgin mountain terrain. Not everyone liked what he built. In 1939 he cut a paved road over a pristine pass near Salida despite protests from the town's citizens. The road was bad enough, but when they heard the governor had decided to name the place Vail Pass, Salidans rebelled. They painted the P out of every Vail Pass sign, and they petitioned the governor to drop the name. He did, renaming it Monarch Pass; Charlie Vail's last name was assigned to a section of newly built U.S. 6 then known as Black Gore Pass.

Twenty years later, when we were thinking up names for our new ski mountain, someone suggested Shining Mountains, the name Ute Indians had given Colorado. I turned it down, because to me shining mountains meant icy mountains.

So the mountain and the resort became Vail after a civil servant who did his level best to pave the Rockies and probably never wore a pair of skis in his life.

★　★　★　★　★

When I think of all that's happened—good, bad, and otherwise—since Earl and I first climbed the mountain, I can hardly believe we survived such tumultuous times. We bought a piece of land in the valley and developed the ski area for $1.5 million; in recent years the value of Vail's stock has reached close to $1 billion. In those early years, we were happy to sell building lots for $4,500 to $9,500; a few years ago a single gas station sold for five times what developing the whole mountain cost us.

In 1970 we celebrated when Colorado was awarded the 1976 Olympic Winter Games. Then aggressive environmentalists who opposed the Games organized a statewide referendum on the issue. Our dream of a Colorado Winter Olympics died.

Horrendous gasoline shortages in the mid 1970s cut deeply into skier days. And in the season of 1980-81, the weather itself left us stoically resigned as snowless day followed snowless day, until we became used to the fact there were often more lift operators and ski patrollers on the mountain than skiers.

The darkest day in all my years at Vail was March 26, 1976, when two cars on the Lionshead gondola got tangled in the cable

Blue Sky Basin was logged off at one time, so the trees—lodgepole pine, spruce, and alpine fir—are widely spaced. That gives the skiing a distinctly backcountry feel.

atop a lift tower and plunged 125 feet to the ground. Four skiers died; eight were badly hurt. The rest of that nightmare day was taken up by heroic ski patrollers bringing down 176 people from the 31 stranded cars. A part of the next decade was taken up with settling the ensuing lawsuits.

The fear of lawsuits led directly to the decision later in 1976 by Vail Associates board members—myself included—to sell the resort for $13 million to a fund controlled by board member Harry Bass, a Texas oil man. From the start Harry and I clashed, and I was eventually forced to leave the company. (I spent the next twelve up-and-down years elsewhere, including at rustic Snowbasin, Utah, and at then-spanking-new Arrowhead in the Vail Valley, which is now part of Vail Resorts.) Eight years later Harry found himself out of a job when the trustees of the fund, including his own children, pulled their money out of Vail because they didn't like the return they were getting on their investment.

The new owner of Vail was a friendly, talkative communications multimillionaire named George Gillett Jr., who had once owned the Harlem Globetrotters, as well as a piece of the Miami Dolphins. When he bought Vail for $130 million in 1985, his fortune was in television stations and meat packing. George was aggressive in expanding and developing the ski area. In my case he was most generous when in 1989 he

Easy and safe access to midwinter solitude is rare in this age of overcrowded cities, pollution, and road rage. Blue Sky Basin offers solitude in abundance.

put me back on the Vail Associates payroll.

In 1992 George Gillett had to sell Vail when he went bankrupt, with debts mounting close to a billion dollars. He was replaced by Apollo Ski Partners, a group of New York investment bankers who created a powerhouse corporation that in 1996 bought two other Colorado ski-area gems—Keystone and Breckenridge—from Ralston Purina. Apollo now rules a skiing kingdom of 10,818 acres served by ninety-one lifts, which attracts a total of 4.5 million skiers each year.

The battle over the development of our luxurious sister resort, Beaver Creek, went on for more than a decade. So has the conflict over the fate of the Canadian lynx, which supposedly had prime habitat where Blue Sky Basin now lies. On October 19, 1998, eco-terrorists set fire to three on-mountain buildings and four chairlifts at Vail in the most violent act of environmental protest ever. The replacement cost was $12 million. Yet the courts ruled that Blue Sky Basin could go forward.

Yes, I have seen my dream child grow into a megaresort. Sometimes I wonder about the MBAs who have replaced us mountain men in running this place. It always pulls me up short when one of these business whizzes uses the word "product" when referring to the skiing at Vail.

But thanks to this "product," I've had a marvelously varied life, met many remarkable people, and had some unlikely experiences. I became friends with the Shah of Iran in 1974 when I spent several weeks on Mount Toschal, outside of Tehran, advising him on building a ski area. He was a pleasant enough fellow, not imperious at all. I also number among my friends President Gerry Ford, Massachusetts Governor Francis Sargent, tennis star Rod Laver, golfer Jack Nicklaus, Congressman Jack Kemp, and some of the greatest skiers of them all, including Jean-Claude Killy, Stein Eriksen, Annemarie Proell, Ingemar Stenmark, and Dick Durrance.

I came within a whisker of being on the cover of *Time* in 1972, when the magazine ran a feature about the world boom in skiing. *Time* photographers took several dozen rolls of film of me, and a correspondent interviewed me day and night for what seemed like a month. However, when the magazine hit the newsstands, on the cover was a beautiful woman who sold skis in Seattle. I was disappointed, but it made me feel better when I saw they had described me in the story as "Peter Seibert, 48, a well-muscled, jovial fellow who has dreamed of building his own ski town ever since he was a ski-crazed little boy in New Hampshire."

I have received many awards and trophies over the years. I've been elected to both the Colorado and National Ski Halls of Fame; was picked as one of the "25 Most Influential People in Skiing" by SKIING Magazine; and was third on SKI Magazine's list of "The 100 Most Influential Skiers." The most unforgettable trophy I was ever given is a bronzed deer penis from the Chinese government, whom I had advised about building a new ski area in northeastern China. They told me it

Most of the terrain in Blue Sky Basin is easy for average skiers and snowboarders to negotiate. But there are also plenty of challenging drops, like this rock launch into Pete's Bowl at Miller's Cliffs.

symbolizes manhood and outdoor expertise. I have kept it on my fireplace mantle ever since.

★ ★ ★ ★ ★

It has been a long and wonderful ride through all these years. In 1996, Vail Resorts was going to replace the Lionshead gondola after twenty-five years, and since I was the one who had had it installed, I was asked to be the last person to ride it up. I was alone in the car. It was an odd and melancholy trip. I couldn't get the images of the 1976 accident out of my mind. I looked out the window to the ground—it seemed a long way to fall.

I had been thinking for a couple of months that I'd like to write a book about my life, but I couldn't seem to get started. I thought of my sons and my grandchildren, my friends from the 10th Mountain Division, my friends from Aspen, and my friends who had come to help me build Vail when it was nothing but a big empty mountain. I watched as the gondola car entered the gloom of the Eagle's Nest terminal. I exited into the sunshine and looked around me at the magnificent views. And I decided then and there that I would somehow produce a book about Vail and my life. Just then I looked up to see an airliner heading west. The contrails looked like two fresh ski tracks streaming across the sky. **V**

NEW ENGLAND YEARS

I was born August 7, 1924, in Sharon, Massachusetts, the first child of Edythe Loring Seibert, 30, and Albert Daniel Seibert, 39. Mother's family, named Monk, had deep roots in Massachusetts. One of her ancestors, Deborah Sampson Gannett, was a Revolutionary heroine—the only woman known to have enlisted and fought with the Continental Army against the British (see box, page 49). Once her wartime exploits were done, Deborah settled in Sharon in 1784, where descendants of the family continued to reside for the next 175 years.

The family was middle-class but quite cultured. My mother graduated from the New England Conservatory of Music in Boston with a major in piano. She was a high-spirited, pretty woman, always cheerful, always humorous and, it seemed, always driving a laughing load of children in our family car. She gave piano lessons to half the children in town. In the evening, she played our grand piano, specializing in Liszt and Chopin.

Mother was also a fine cook, and I got my first hint that cooking might be an art form when she and her mother, Mrs. Laura D. White Monk, took over the restaurant at the Blue Hill Country Club in Canton, Massachusetts. Though they didn't produce gourmet fare by today's standards—they were, after all, devout disciples of Fanny Farmer—I recall with a watering mouth their delicious poached chicken and crisp home-grown vegetables, followed by mouth-melting lemon meringue and mincemeat pies.

My father was born in Roslindale, Massachusetts, to a successful German family that owned a small chain of delicatessens in the Boston area. He was the first of six siblings and possessed some remarkable talents: He had perfect pitch and could play any piece on the piano after hearing it just once. As a boy, I was convinced my dad was the equal to Mozart.

He was also a fine painter, in both oil and watercolor. He particularly admired the French impressionists Corot and Cézanne as well as the great German landscape painter Albert Bierstadt, who specialized in majestic oil paintings of the American West. My father also loved the powerful sculptures Frederic Remington did of horses and cowboys.

My father's life changed dramatically in the spring of 1900, when his father died, leaving a widow, six children, and financial problems. At just sixteen, my father was forced to become the head and sole supporter of the household. He gave up all plans for his own education beyond high school, instead working at every job he could find. Eventually he and his mother managed to put the five other children through college. When the last of them finished school in 1909, my dad was twenty-five. At that point he was ready to begin his own life—and what a life it was.

Besides his great abilities as a pianist and painter, my father also possessed a passion for physical challenge and an irresistible wanderlust. So he headed west to see in the flesh Remington's noble

Behind the Seibert home at 195 East Street, Sharon, Massachusetts, was the family barn, where, at age seven, Pete discovered a pair of maple-wood skis that had belonged to his mother when she was young. Those skis ignited his passion for the sport.

Above: Ranch hand, gold miner, engineer, salesman, Albert Daniel Seibert, Pete's father, was a man of prodigious talents. He could paint landscapes in oil or water-color from memory and play virtually any tune on the piano after hearing it just once. Below: Albert panning gold in Miami, Arizona, 1913.

cowpokes and Beirstadt's stunning mountains. He found a willing companion, his cousin Peter Werner (my namesake), who owned a Model T Ford. They just took off, traversing what was only the beginning of the eventual network of passable roads for the automobile. The more rugged the landscape, the more they liked it. They crossed the Midwest, the Rocky Mountains, and the Arizona desert, before Arizona was a state.

They went as far as the West Coast and Southern California, and decided to settle there for a while, working as ranch hands. As it turned out, Dad loved the job, and he stayed on. Peter Werner, however, drove up the coast to San Francisco, sold his trusty Model T, and booked passage back to Boston through the newly finished Panama Canal.

Soon enough, though, my father's wanderlust took over. He left California, moved to Arizona, and spent several years working as a cowboy on a ranch near Tucson. But he was fascinated by the Rocky Mountains. He eventually went north to

Colorado and worked in the San Luis Valley, around Alamosa, as a ranch hand. Later he took a job mining gold and silver in Leadville, just about thirty miles from where Vail is today. He lived in a small settlement called Stump Town, which was run by the mining company and offered rough lodging and bare-fisted entertainment. Father told me often of the times Jack Dempsey, several years away from the heavyweight championship and fighting under the name Kid Blackie, would arrive in Leadville, offer to take on all comers, and go home with a few bucks.

Stump Town was a dangerous place, not only because of the hard-knuckle fights that went on but also because mining itself was a brutal business that took countless lives. Sometime around 1920, my father had his jaw broken in a mine cave-in while working underground. He barely escaped alive. He viewed the experience as a painful omen to give up his roustabout life in Stump Town and return to the genteel world of Sharon.

* * * * *

I enjoyed a New England childhood that was like growing up in a Norman Rockwell painting. We lived on a five-acre plot with a large lawn and fruit trees, a slightly run-down hundred-year-old white Victorian house, and a faded red barn. In summer, we had a swimming hole in Mann's Pond, next to my grandfather's textile mill.

Our house was located near three of the most notable landmarks in Sharon: the nine-hole Sharon Golf Club; Geissler's Farm, which was famous statewide for its apple cider; and the nudist colony, where a couple of hundred naked souls spent summers living together in tents.

Nudes notwithstanding, winter was my favorite season.

The first time I ever touched a pair of skis, I was seven years old. The great moment occurred while I was rummaging around among the hay bales and the worn-out harnesses stored in the loft of our barn. In a dark corner, apparently unnoticed for years, stood a pair of maple-wood skis, things of beauty and wonderment despite the dust that covered them. It turned out they belonged to my mother. They had been carefully shaped and carved by a local woodworker especially for her. But she had given up the sport after she had children, and I inherited the skis. Never have I experienced a more complete sense of joy and adventure than when I first stuck my hunting boots into the leather toe straps and proceeded down the modest hills outside town. My life changed completely because of those first real skis.

Edith Loring Seibert, Pete's mother, taught piano lessons to half the children in Sharon, Massachusetts, ran a restaurant, and raised two children.

For the next couple of years, no one was happier than me as I progressed from shallow open slopes to steep, tree-filled ones and then to homemade ski jumps that sent me hurtling fifteen or twenty feet through the air. When I was nine, my parents astounded me at Christmas with a mighty pair of seven-foot-long pine skis. From my height of four and a half feet or so, those things looked as high as the telegraph poles that ran along the railroad tracks. But I mastered them, too, and my mother's skis went to my sister, Christine, two years younger than me.

Besides delivering my greatest thrills, skis also delivered the greatest heartbreak I ever suffered as a child. In our efforts to find challenges on snowy hills, we kids had shoveled a ramp up to a large tree stump in the woods, the takeoff point for our longest ski jump yet. The landing area was not large, and the snow was hard packed. I flung myself off the stump, flew majestically (or so I thought) toward the landing, and then hit the ground heavily and fell. My left ski had snapped in half where the wood was mortised for the toe strap.

Determined to make that jump, I next convinced my sister to let me borrow the precious maple skis. I came speeding down the approach, rose off the stump too high, looked down at the world, then hit the icy landing. There was a sharp clap of skis followed by a snapping sound. My sister began to cry. To my despair, I saw that the tip of the right ski had broken off.

A bleak realization dawned: We were without a usable pair of skis, and the winter wasn't even half over. New skis cost twenty dollars a pair, a fortune at that time. It took me a full summer of woodcutting and lawn mowing, at thirty-five cents an hour, until I could buy secondhand skis, which were far shorter than my majestic seven footers.

* * * * *

On winter evenings we skated on a nearby pond. We would light a roaring fire, let it burn to hot coals, then roast potatoes.

We played hockey with rolled magazines under our pants' legs to protect our shins, using a small round rock as a puck and larger stones to mark the goal.

But life wasn't just one long delicious ski run followed by another high-spirited hockey game. I can barely remember a time from childhood on when I didn't work, particularly in the summer, to save money for my future education. Shoveling snow, chopping wood, weeding gardens, mowing lawns, stacking grocery shelves, picking corn, putting up hay—I scarcely ever had a day off and never made more than ninety cents an hour. Those jobs seemed hard at the time, but none was as exhausting or as excruciating as the work I did in the summer of 1940, at age sixteen, as an apprentice boilermaker repairing rusted-out railroad cars. The boilermaker's main task was to replace the floor plates or splash plates in coal cars and tank cars. In hundred-degree heat we worked with deafening rivet guns and red-hot rivets that sent up boiling clouds of steam when they came in contact with water in the cars. It was a sweltering, ear-splitting job.

I worked seven days a week, ten hours each weekday, eight hours per day on weekends. I was paid maybe ninety cents an hour, and I allowed myself exactly one dollar a week to spend on soda pop (a nickel) and candy bars (also a nickel). The rest I saved for college.

But I was sixteen and strong for my age. I even held another job simultaneously, as caretaker of the Sharon Tennis Club's two clay courts. No money changed hands, but I had the right to play for free. Often on weekends I would play two or three ferocious sets with my best pal, Irv Post, after putting in eight hours at the car works first.

When our family later moved to North Conway, New Hampshire, Irv visited during the summers and we worked as golf-course caddies at the Eastern Slopes Inn, a popular resort in North Conway that sometimes attracted celebrities. The most dazzling guest of them all was Yankee slugger Babe Ruth. One day Irv and I were playing a fierce game of tennis and the Babe himself sat down near the court and began cheering for me. Perhaps because I was shorter and my game was less polished than Irv's, Ruth had picked me as an underdog worth rooting for. Irv was irked—so much so that he lost the match.

The next day Ruth was part of a foursome for which the two

> When winter skies are drab and gray
> Then, Jack Frost goes his icy way
> But stops, to etch upon the pane
> His promise, that in spring again,
> The ferns and grass and trailing vines,
> Will come to life beneath the pines.
> And where we now see drifted snow
> We'll see again the flowers grow.
>   Dad.

Above: Writing poetry was another of Albert Seibert's many talents. Below: When snow fell at the Stanton Farm in Bartlett, New Hampshire, Pete (far right) and his cousins had themselves a backyard ski slope, complete with rope tow.

By 1941, at age seventeen, Pete was winning local and regional races in New England and finding acrobatic ways to shake the sticky snow off his ski bases.

of us were caddying. The Sultan of Swat not only had a caddy to carry his golf bag but also a second one to pull a small wagon loaded with bottles of gin and tonic. We kids, firm abstainers when it came to "demon rum," were disgusted by the great Babe's pathetic slide into decadence. We both agreed that he was over the hill.

* * * * *

We lived in Sharon until the late 1930s, but the Depression was taking its toll on our family finances. Ultimately, my father volunteered to work year-round for the Civilian Conservation Corps, a government program that put otherwise jobless men to work building parks, beaches, hiking trails, and shelters in the magnificent American wilderness. Father's job as a civil engineer and maker of relief maps took him to Bartlett, New Hampshire. To be near him in the summers, Mother, Christine, and I rented a farmhouse on the hills above town. Eventually, his absences became too painful, and we left Sharon to live full time in New Hampshire.

It was a boon to my skiing, I can tell you that. In our backyard were wide open slopes and a rope tow. Our own rope tow! We probably lived in one of the first ski-in/ ski-out homes in the U.S. I began winning local ski races when I was fifteen. Soon I had even mastered that steepest of skiers' paradises: Tuckerman Ravine on Mount Washington.

For the next several years, I was a tiger on the hill—tough, grim, and determined to win every competition I could. At the time, I thought winning ski races was the ultimate test of ability and spirit. God, how wonderful if that were true. Entirely too soon I would learn the truth about human nature in response to real conflict. **V**⦾

REVOLUTIONARY DEBORAH

One of my ancestors, Deborah Sampson Gannett, was directly related to the founding fathers. Her mother was Deborah Bradford, great granddaughter of William Bradford, governor of Plymouth Colony, and her great grandfather was married to Lydia Standish, a granddaughter of Myles Standish.

But even the best of bloodlines don't guarantee a happy life. And, in

Deborah Sampson Gannett

truth, revered Deborah Sampson suffered as a child. Her father deserted the family when she was ten, and her impoverished mother was forced to send all her children away as indentured servants. Deborah did barnyard chores for a number of farm families. She managed to teach herself to read and write and also mastered the craft of sewing her own clothes. At seventeen she began to teach in the public schools of Middleboro, Massachusetts. Then, at age twenty -one, in the year 1782, when the war was about four years along, she made a strange and inexplicable decision: She would disguise herself as a man and enlist in the Revolutionary Army.

She sewed herself a stylish outfit—coat, waistcoat, breeches, etc.—that fit her manly height of five feet, seven inches. She compressed her breasts in bandages and became a smooth-faced young man named Robert Shurtlieff. For the next year and a half, she fought in several historic battles, including Yorktown where the British Army, under Lord Cornwallis, was brought to surrender.

No one saw through her disguise. Once in a battle at Tarrytown she took a bullet in the shoulder. Instead of risking a hospital visit where her sex might be revealed, she treated the wounds herself— leaving the bullet implanted in her shoulder for the rest of her life.

In April 1783, General John Patterson, commander at West Point, selected her as his aide-de-camp, because he was impressed by "this soldier's heroism and fidelity." Two months later she was sent to Philadelphia on a special mission for the general. She contracted a terrible fever and could barely stand or talk when she arrived. She was hospitalized, and her secret was discovered.

She returned to West Point, and General Patterson demanded, "Is it true you are a woman?"

"What will be my fate if I confess it?" she asked.

"You have nothing to fear," said the gentle general.

Whereupon the young woman burst into tears and fainted. She returned to Sharon and married Benjamin Gannett Jr. in 1784. She was always treated as a heroine instead of a sexual outcast. She gave lectures about her life as a woman in the Revolutionary Army. In 1818, impoverished and old, she applied to Congress for an army pension. After much debate, she was granted eight dollars a month.

She died in 1827. Her statue stands in Sharon, Massachusetts.

CHAPTER FOUR

THE WAR YEARS

In late May 1943, I left New England on a troop train for Pando, Colorado, which was not far from Leadville, scene of one of my father's Western adventures. My destination was Camp Hale, an instant city of more than eight hundred buildings constructed by the army in the valley of the Eagle River. This was the training site of the newly formed 10th Mountain Division of skiing soldiers.

As Pearl Harbor had been bombed in December 1941 and the war effort was building, I had assumed I would soon be going into the service. But the draft board had given me a school deferment, and I spent a year taking a college prep course at New Hampton School in New Hampshire. After I graduated in 1943, I expected my army draft notice to be issued any day. I initially preferred the navy air corps, so I got the application papers from a navy recruiter and filled them out. But when I went to return them, a line of applicants snaked all the way around the building. So I went to see the army recruiter instead and quickly volunteered for the 10th Mountain Division. With the help of the National Ski Patrol, the army was looking for good skiers. I was chosen for the division and went directly to Camp Hale.

The camp consisted of row upon row of freshly constructed living quarters for some sixteen thousand officers and men, plus stables for four thousand horses and mules. Black smoke billowed over the countryside from the coal-burning stoves and furnaces used to heat the hundreds of barracks. This was made even denser by the clouds of smoke that belched from the trains that hauled men and materials in and out of Camp Hale every day. A constant smog hung low over the valley, and soot often covered every surface, including rifles, tents, and uniforms. This pervasive air pollution caused respiratory ailments among thousands of 10th Mountain recruits—everything from the common cold to fatal pneumonia.

There were other hazards at Camp Hale, including the world's first snowcats, called Weasels, which had been specially designed for maneuvering in snowy mountain terrain. But they were also dangerously top-heavy, and dozens of soldiers suffered serious injuries when the cats turned over without warning. Frostbite was also a problem. A huge training maneuver in March 1944, called the D-series, required nine thousand of us to hike into the wilds to altitudes of thirteen thousand feet and

Previous page: 10th Mountain troops

at Cooper Hill near Camp Hale, 1943-44

undertake three continuous weeks of war games. At one point a horrendous blizzard hit and the snowdrifts rose to fifteen feet, making it impossible for mules or horses to move. Temperatures fell to minus thirty-five, radio batteries froze, and at least a hundred men were evacuated in a single day with frostbite. We would later joke that combat against the Germans was almost as bad as D-series training.

Many of our men were from warmer climates and knew nothing about skis, snow, or climbing sheer walls of rock. They had difficulty mastering the mountaineering skills they were being taught. Putting up tents seemed an impossible dream. And once a tent was up, the snow melted around it, soaking tent, sleeping bag, and occupant. In subzero temperatures, the danger of freezing to death was very real.

The expert skiers among us tried to teach these lowlanders the rudiments of skiing—mainly snowplows and stem turns. Just as some of them were beginning to get the idea, however, the camp commander ordered everyone to carry rifles and rucksacks for all training drills, heavy snow or not. This resulted in yet another problem: When the poor beginners toppled over into the deep powder snow that fell constantly during that winter of 1943-44, they floundered helplessly like turtles on their backs. They had to fight so hard merely to get to their feet that some became utterly enfeebled and had to be admitted to a field hospital.

Opposite: Pete wearing his summer battle dress: army-issue, ankle-high boots; canvas leggings; wool pants; reversible parka; M1 rifle; rucksack with sleeping bag; first-aid kit; extra clothing; rations; and, on his head, steel helmet with helmet liner. Below: Camp Hale from Yoder Gulch, summer of 1943, when sixteen-thousand mountain troopers lived here.

Another part of the Camp Hale routine was the care and feeding of the animals—hundreds of horses and mules that were used to haul equipment and guns on our training journeys into the backcountry. Stable duty was not a favorite assignment, but we managed to make some fun out of it. I was once mucking out the mules' stalls with Steve Knowlton, my best friend in the division and a fellow New Englander who would go on to have a major postwar influence on skiing in Colorado. We were working in the manure with shovel and rake when the bugler began to play retreat. When the bugle sounded, we were all supposed to stop what we were doing and present arms with our rifles. Steve and I hesitated, then quickly snapped to attention and presented the arms we had at hand—rake and shovel. Someone saw us and turned us in. We had to do KP (kitchen patrol) for the next month.

Above: Pete in the backcountry above Camp Hale during training, shortly before being shipped to Camp Swift in Texas, early spring 1944. Pete is wearing his own glacier glasses, which cost about fifteen dollars (half a month's pay). Below: Learning to ski on seven-foot, three-inch skis with a heavy pack on was not easy. Besides that, many troops were flatlanders who had never seen snow.

* * * * *

As it turned out, we didn't spend all of our time training in a winter environment. After those punishing months in the cold at Camp Hale, we were sent to Camp Swift, Texas, which some of us assumed would be an improvement. To our amazement, though, things were even worse: 120-degree heat, jungle

training, twenty-five mile forced marches carrying the prescribed ninety pound packs. We began to think we might be training for assaults on volcanic islands in the South Pacific or perhaps Burma, which was mountainous and hot. But that wasn't the case, and, as usual, the army never explained or apologized for the absurdities it laid on its long-suffering soldiers.

As it happened, the 10th Mountain Division's major combat missions took place in the Italian Alps. Our first mission, in mid February 1945, called for a treacherous nighttime climb up sheer cliffs that led to German observation positions on Riva Ridge, in the Apennines north of Florence. If we took Riva, we would be in position to attack heavily defended Mount Belvedere, a thirty-eight hundred foot peak that was an important part of a German defensive line blocking invasion routes into the Po River Valley, where German arms were manufactured. Both the U.S. Fifth and British Eighth Armies had been trying for months to punch through this Gothic line. Now a single division of well-trained but untried mountaineers and skiers was going to try to achieve what two armies had not.

I was a platoon sergeant in charge of forty men. For more than a week we scouted Riva Ridge, rock by rock. We established where the Germans had dug in on top, and we found routes that allowed us to move men and weapons up to attack and occupy the ridge in one night. The climbs ranged from fifteen hundred to twenty-two hundred feet—no Sunday afternoon excursions, I can tell you.

At 10 P.M. on the night of February 18, 1945, we headed toward the base of Riva. Ours was the lead unit, Company F of the

HOW ELITE WAS THE 10TH?

Swiss Walter Prager, who was the Dartmouth ski coach before World War II, proved to have magnificent foresight when he said, "Thousands of GIs who skied for the 10th Mountain Division are going to play a big part in the new ski industry boom that is about to burst over this country."

It was true: No less than two thousand 10th Mountain vets became ski instructors and ski patrolmen. Eventually 10th Mountain men were practically running American skiing. Here's a partial list:

- **Fritz Benedict** was an architect and developer in Aspen.
- **Nelson Bennett** managed White Pass, Washington.
- **Bill "Sarge" Brown** was mountain manager at Vail.
- **Curt Chase** was director of the Aspen Ski School.
- **Bil Dunaway** was editor of SKIING Magazine and publisher of the Aspen Times.
- **Ralph "Doc" Des Roches** was executive director of Ski Industries of America.
- **Ben Duke** was on the board of Vail Associates.
- **Paul Duke** was manager at Breckenridge, Colorado.
- **Alf Engen** directed the ski school at Alta, Utah.
- **Luggi Foeger** directed the ski school at Badger Pass, California.
- **Merrill Hastings** founded SKIING Magazine.
- **Bill Healy** created Mt. Bachelor, Oregon.
- **Nick Hock** was associate publisher of SKI Magazine.
- **Dev Jennings** was executive director of Ski New England.
- **Dave Judson** founded Otis Ridge, Massachusetts.
- **Larry Jump** was president of Arapahoe Basin, Colorado.
- **Steve Knowlton** was the first executive director of Colorado Ski Country USA.
- **Ed Link** founded Crystal Mountain, Washington.
- **John Litchfield** was co-director of the Aspen Ski School.
- **Dick May** managed Wildcat, New Hampshire.
- **Jack Murphy** founded Sugarbush, Vermont.
- **Bob Nordhaus** created Sandia Peak, New Mexico.
- **Bob Parker** was editor of SKIING Magazine and Vail's first marketing director.
- **Bud Phillips** directed the ski school at Mad River Glen, Vermont.
- **Friedl Pfeifer** directed the Aspen Ski School and created Buttermilk Mountain.
- **Percy Rideout** was co-director of the Aspen Ski School.
- **Kerr Sparks** directed the ski school at Stowe, Vermont.
- **Clif Taylor** promoted the Graduated Length Method (GLM) of ski instruction.
- **Thad Thorne** managed Attitash, New Hampshire.
- **Laverne Trepp** founded Pine Mountain, Michigan.
- **Jack Tweedy** was a vice president and attorney of the Vail Corporation.
- **Dick Wilson** was editor of SKIING Magazine.
- **Gordon Wren** directed the Loveland Basin Ski School and was manager at Steamboat, Colorado.

John Litchfield wearing his hand-knit wool sweater with distinctive skunk pattern.

Tenth Mountain troopers from Camp Hale often spent their free time skiing in Aspen. This group stands in front of the Hotel Jerome, home to a famous mixed drink called the Aspen Crud, made with two shots of whiskey in a milkshake.

The climb took more than five hours. Despite sporadic gunfire, we kept moving until we reached the top, where we dug shelters in the snowbanks along the ridge. Now daylight was dawning, but a dense morning fog lay over the mountains. It made a perfect cover for our advance on the German positions. As we moved across Riva, we spotted fleeing shadows in the fog. The German soldiers, confused and frightened, didn't know what to do when they realized the Americans had

86th Regiment, and we proceeded silently, under starless skies, toward a river crossing made of rocks. We were carrying heavy packs and extra ammunition. Some men were having trouble keeping their balance on the crossing; a few fell in. I managed to get some logs to make a more stable bridge. Then I jumped into the icy, waist-deep water to guide those who needed help. One rifleman had fallen in a deep part of the river, and he was soaked through. He retreated to the south shore and refused to try to cross again. I was wet and very cold myself, but took the shivering soldier back to a farmhouse that was being used as an aid station. There I changed into dry socks, went back to cross the river on the bridge of logs, and hurried to catch my men, who were slowly—and silently—ascending the cliffs leading to the ridge.

Everyone was laboring under the burden of packs and ammo. Men were panting and wheezing. If the Germans detected our attack while we were on the cliffs, they could probably wipe us out. But I fought off my fear by concentrating on being utterly silent and by repeating in my mind the precise details of what my men and I had to do once we hit the top.

arrived. They had believed themselves safe from any attack from below. Their outposts were scattered about and lightly manned, and their gun emplacements were not designed to beat back an assault.

By early afternoon my platoon's section of the ridge had been thoroughly searched and secured. The enemy had fled. Other members of the 86th Regiment, spread out along the three-and-a-half-mile ridge, were not so lucky; some of them endured four days of persistent German counterattacks. Our engineers to the northeast constructed a cable line from the base to the top, allowing us to lift both men and supplies across the river and up the steep face that had taken all night to climb.

The attack on Riva Ridge was a triumph for the 86th Mountain Regiment. We had succeeded at one of the most difficult maneuvers in the military textbooks. The assault on Mount Belvedere came two days later, with the 85th and 87th carrying the brunt. We of the 86th were rewarded with a few days of R&R in a small village, Vidiciatico, at the base of Belvedere. A couple of us went skiing—for fun! The snow was perfectly softened from the sun, and we took looping run after run. We even put sticks in the snow to mark a slalom course. None of us was exactly in Olympic form—we were wearing mountain combat boots and skiing on army-issue skis that were seven-feet, three-inches long—but we had plenty of wine to keep us going. Later I realized that those days in early March were the last time I ever skied on two good legs.

Ironically, that wine-filled ski slope at Vidiciatico gave us front row seats to watch the fighting on Mount Belvedere, not more than ten miles away across a valley. As if watching a newsreel, we saw American planes bomb and strafe the topmost ridges, where the Germans were dug in. Ultimately, this battle proved to be key to breaking through the German's Gothic line and made possible all subsequent victories.

General George P. Hays, our commanding officer, sent a letter of commendation to the officers and men of the 10th that read: "You accomplished all of your assigned missions with magnificent dash and determination. You caught the enemy completely by surprise. You over-ran and defeated elements of eight different enemy battalions, from which you captured four hundred prisoners of war.

"By your action, you have won the confidence and admiration of all troops within the theatre and the highest praise of

After months of strenuous and almost continuous training at altitudes above 10,000 feet, the 10th Mountain troops, such as this contingent near Mitchell Creek above Camp Hale, were among the best-trained soldiers in the army. Even the German war planners had heard of them.

your corps, army group, and deputy theatre commanders."

Two months later, our troops received an even more impressive letter of commendation from General Mark Clark, the commander of all troops in Italy, who wrote to the commander of the Fifth Army: "Your units, spearheaded by the gallant 10th Mountain Division, have dealt the enemy a staggering blow. The 10th Mountain Division, which entered the line only last January, has performed with outstanding skill and strength. The German forces are reeling from your quick assaults."

The troopers in the 10th Mountain Division not only worked and trained together—they also socialized together. Here Pete (second from right) has a drink with 10th Mountain buddies in a Chicago bar on his way back to Camp Hale from a two-week leave to visit his parents. Many 10th friendships lasted a lifetime.

* * * * *

After the conquest at Belvedere, we were sent to fight in another range of mountains to the northeast. The battle for Mount Terminale began in early March. On March 3, 1945, my platoon was acting as the advance column on the south flank of Terminale. As we moved carefully ahead, we saw the bodies of Americans and Germans strewn about the mountainside. I passed a badly wounded young German who was pleading for someone to kill him. I moved by him and a moment later heard a single shot behind me. I didn't turn around to see who had fired it.

We were approaching a particularly well-defended point in the German line, and I ordered the platoon to halt and wait for our support units to move up on our flanks. Far below in the valley, I could see a U.S. tank maneuvering to cross a small stone bridge, and I wondered idly about the Roman legions who had built that bridge while they, too, possibly were at war in these mountains.

Later that afternoon the German bombardment had increased. I was standing near a farmhouse that gave some small protection when I heard the familiar voice of Steve Knowlton. He had been separated from his unit on night patrol, and he was working his way back to it. We exchanged brief remarks about the intensity of the German mortar fire. After Steve left, the Germans began shelling even more heavily in our direction. Within minutes, I was hit.

I heard a deafening blast and saw stars in many colors, the predominant one being bright red. A mortar shell had exploded in a small oak tree just above my head. The tree then had burst apart in a violent rain of splintered wood and fragments of mortar shell. The first pain came from my shattered left forearm, which felt as if it had been hit with a baseball bat. I tried to stand up, but my right leg was useless, and I fell back. I gazed into the face of Sergeant Hutchens, another platoon leader in F Company. He was yelling words I know he didn't believe: "You'll be okay, Pete. Lie back, you're okay." It was about then that I realized that I'd also been hit in the face. I was spitting teeth, gagging and choking on the blood in my throat.

I tried to elevate my smashed arm to slow the flow of blood. Sergeant Hutchens moved away. Two buddies came by, looked at me, and left without speaking. I wondered if I was already dead. It occurred to me that I had promised these two pals several personal items of value if I was killed: my wallet, a sheath knife, an automatic pistol, a mess kit, and my watch. I removed my watch from my elevated left arm with my right hand and discovered that I had been hit in the fingers of that hand, too. I tried to conceal the watch and my wallet under my shirt. As I did so I found that blood from two chest wounds was pouring

When soldiers moved to take up new positions, the standing order was, "Don't bunch up." These troops are moving up the slopes of Mount Belvedere after one of the fiercest battles of the Italian campaign.

onto my stomach and congealing.

Suddenly my good friend and platoon medic, Howie Schless, appeared at my side. He was shooting me with morphine, and he too was saying, "You'll make it, Pete." Before I could reply, there was another tremendous blast. I felt helpless, lost, hopeless, and alone. An instant later I realized that Howie's right shoulder had been blown apart by this second mortar shell. He had been working less than a foot from my head.

The force of the blast spun Howie around, but he managed to return to my side. His first reaction was to put his hand over his mouth and suck in his breath to find out if his lungs had been punctured. He gasped, "My lungs are okay, Pete." He then began to check my wounds but had been hit too hard. He collapsed on the ground, bleeding terribly. Two other medics carried him away on a field stretcher.

I have no idea how long I lay there. The heavy dose of morphine had kicked in. I was floating. I didn't even know that the second mortar blast had smashed my right leg in the calf. I remember trying to crawl under some downed trees when another medic came to lie beside me to provide cover.

Later I was carried by two medics on a bouncing litter. The trip was over rough terrain, and the pain was growing despite the morphine. At one point, the medics put me down in a protected place as shells exploded within yards of us. Finally, we made it to the battalion aid station set up in a farmhouse. As we went in, I saw two jeeps parked in the courtyard. The medics lifted me onto the kitchen table to dress my wounds. A couple of times shells actually hit the farmhouse, and the medics were forced to lower me to a safer place under the table. They huddled there, too, waiting for the shell fire to ease up.

Finally they finished my emergency dressings, put me back on the litter, and dashed into the courtyard. One of the two jeeps was overturned and burning. The driver and his mechanic lay dead on the ground. I was loaded on the remaining jeep and held down on the litter by two ashen-faced medics as we bounced over rutted country roads to get out of bombardment range.

* * * * *

My next stop was the regiment aid station, much like the MASH hospitals seen on TV. I was operated on, stitched up, and pumped full of morphine and penicillin. In bandaging my mutilated face, the doctors had covered both eyes. I could see nothing, but the moans and coughs and shouts of my fellow patients came through loud and clear. So did the soothing voices of the nurses, who fed me through a tube and gave me penicillin shots eight times a day in my right shoulder—one of the few parts of my body that hadn't been damaged by mortar fire.

My wounds were profound but not quite catastrophic. The first shell, which had exploded in the tree over my head, blew fragments of shrapnel through the front of my helmet, splitting my nose open and knocking out my front teeth. Other fragments from the same shell had almost severed my left arm at the elbow and had smashed into my right knee, destroying the kneecap and breaking the head of the femur. A second shell had hit me in the chest and the calf of my right leg, at the same time that it tore off Howie Schless's shoulder joint.

I don't remember anything about my move from the aid station to the army hospital in Livorno. I just woke up there one day in a bed with clean sheets. My face was rebandaged so I could see out of one eye. These were great improvements, but my left arm had become seriously infected and the poisons were coursing through my system. It took a month of powerful doses of penicillin for the infection to subside and for me to begin feeling better. I remember waking up and watching a soldier struggling to hobble down the corridor between beds. "Look at that poor bastard," I remarked to the fellow in the bed next to me.

He looked at me, then said quietly, "You're the poor bastard, Pete. At least he is up and moving around. You can't even move."

I refused, however, to see myself as more pitiful than anyone else or consider that I might die or become a permanent cripple. For a long time, I looked like I was near death. I couldn't walk or even sit up. But my will to live was strong.

I spent almost two months in the Livorno hospital. By then I was able to sit up in a wheelchair for short periods of time. I could manage to feed myself occasionally with my bandaged right hand, but I was unable to do much else.

I was put then on a hospital ship bound for the navy base at Hampton Roads, Virginia. A window was cut in the plaster cast on my right leg so the dressings could be changed on my wound, which was still open and draining after all that time. We spent fourteen days on the ship, a nightmare voyage of men groaning with pain and screaming in their sleep. Many men were seasick, and many of us weren't able to bathe aboard the ship. The stench of our wounds was overwhelming at times. Plus we couldn't move out of our bunks to go up on deck, and there was no fresh air in the compartments.

We arrived at Hampton Roads on a warm, sunny morning in May. We were carried off the ship on litters and laid down in ranks on a dock. Each of us wore a tag marked with our name and destination—not unlike luggage waiting to be picked up at an airport. I remember nothing more of that day except that I ended up in Martinsburg, West Virginia, in an army hospital that specialized in orthopedic medicine.

I was limited to moving about in a wheelchair. I couldn't use crutches because of the large cast on my left arm. The first day, as I was rolled into the mess hall, I saw Howie Schless, the medic who was wounded while caring for me in Italy. He was walking but had a huge shoulder cast that went down to his waist. I wondered how he could sleep at night. A problem for all the recovering wounded was how to get comfortable enough to sleep.

The function of the doctors and nurses at this hospital was mainly to make us ambulatory and to treat our other wounds as required. Besides Howie, I found another friend from the 86th, Danny Orlosky from New Jersey. He had a bad leg wound that wouldn't heal. The doctors kept it open in hopes that it would stop draining. It didn't. After two months, Danny was sent to Walter Reed hospital in Washington, where they amputated his leg below the knee. I never saw him again.

I spent six months in Martinsburg and eventually was able to walk, though I had a pronounced limp. We had a social life of sorts there. On weekend passes to town, we used to stop at the home of a farmer/bootlegger. He would ask us politely what brand of hooch we preferred, and we would reply Jack Daniels or Wild Turkey or Seagrams 7. He would say, "Coming right up." Then he would go into his cellar, find empty bottles with the right labels, fill them all from the same barrel of rotgut and charge us ten dollars for a fifth. We didn't care, though. We carried the bottle in a brown paper bag and

*After the victory of Riva Ridge, the troops of Pete's 86th Mountain Regiment were rewarded
with a few days of R&R in the village of Vidiciatico. The dedicated skiers among them set a
makeshift course and ran slalom while the battle for Mount Belvedere raged just a few miles away.*

nipped on it while we drank beer in the local bars, which were not allowed to sell hard liquor.

Finally, in October 1945, I was allowed a week-long home visit to Sharon. My family had moved back to Massachusetts from New Hampshire shortly before the last peace treaties were signed. Postwar prosperity was already underway. My jack-of-all-trades father had brought forward another talent no one knew he had: working as a truck-fleet salesman. At the age of sixty-one, he went to work for the Dodge Motor Company in melting-pot Boston as a multilanguage huckster who sold almost as many vehicles in Spanish, Yiddish, and German as he did in English.

I don't remember how I got home from Martinsburg, but I do vividly recall that I limped up the lawn with a tear or two rolling down my smiling face. Mother was terribly stricken when she first saw me coming across the lawn. She thought I had crippled both legs because my combat boots with strap-on cuffs looked to her like orthopedic devices. Father was stunned by the display of scars and bandages on my face. He thought I would be disfigured for life.

Soon after I returned to Martinsburg, I was transferred to the Valley Forge army hospital near Phoenixville, Pennsylvania. There I underwent ten months of plastic surgery and pretty much ended up looking like I had before I was hit—except a little older and a bit wiser.

I had spent thirty-nine months in the army, seventeen of them in hospitals. I had been told over and over that I might not walk again and that, certainly, I would never ski. I was released from the army in August 1946, the month I turned twenty-two. I returned to Sharon, worked for the town road department, and drank a lot of beer with high school buddies. But my dream was clear: One way or another, skiing was going to be my life. And I was going to start in Aspen, Colorado. This new American mecca for skiers was about to open in four months. I couldn't wait. ▣

CHAPTER FIVE

COLORADO DAYS

By the winter of 1947-48, Pete's war-torn right leg, with its homemade brace, was beginning to get stronger. But he still made better right turns than left turns.

I took a train west from New England to Glenwood Springs in early September 1946 and hitched a ride on a coal truck going to Aspen. I had skied there many times on weekend passes from Camp Hale in 1943 and 1944. A group of us would pay one dollar each to the owner of a car to drive us the 220 miles to Aspen and back to Camp Hale. We'd sleep and eat at the famous old Hotel Jerome—one dollar for a room, a dollar-fifty for a Sunday prime rib dinner with violin and piano accompaniment.

The Jerome was for decades just about the classiest hotel west of the Mississippi River. When it opened in 1889, this three-story red-brick pile of elegance featured hot running water, electric lights, a water-powered elevator, a greenhouse, a French chef, a livery stable, and a barbershop. Room rates were higher in those days than when I stayed there fifty years later.

As early as 1935, skiers were transported in a miner's truck from the Jerome up the back side of Aspen Mountain on old mining roads to the Midnight Mine. From there, they would strap on skins, hike to the top, and fling themselves joyously down the face of Aspen Mountain or Little Annie Basin. Another form of transport up the hill was the "boat tow," a device that pulled eight skiers at a time to the bottom of "the Corkscrew" at the base of Roch Run. The "boat" was made from parts of discarded mining equipment and ran about four hundred vertical feet up the mountain, giving us a good slalom slope on which to practice technique and creating some exciting bumps at the bottom of the downhill course.

Aspen had been a skiing wonderland for us back in army days, but now I felt I had arrived at the absolute center of the

Above: Life in Aspen in those early days was not without humor. Pete's mom, reading the book, ignores a bobcat attack. Below: "Forget cleaning off the car, Mabel, we're going powder skiing!"

★ ★ ★ ★ ★

As the winter of 1946–47 loomed over us, I secured a job on the ski patrol for the season. I told the head of the patrol, my 10th Mountain buddy Curt Chase, that I was sure I could ski with my wounded right knee and my numb left hand. In fact, there wasn't much I hadn't done already, including the toughest and most demanding kind of physical labor at high altitudes throughout the fall. Nevertheless I had not skied since the first mortar shell hit me on Mount Terminale nineteen months before.

Throughout November we built and equipped patrol headquarters next to the Sundeck restaurant at the top of Aspen Mountain. We set up a primitive phone system using army-surplus phones. We also stowed toboggans and first-aid material up and down the hill and, at the same time, packed down the early snow on the trails. Accomplishing the latter required day after day of sidestepping up and down the full 3,200 vertical feet of the mountain through

skiing universe. The longest chairlift in the world was going up. Some of the best trails ever to grace a mountain were being sculpted and cleared on Aspen: Ruthie's Run, Spar Gulch, Silver Queen. It seemed as if every great skier in the U.S. was there, many of whom were my colleagues from the 10th Mountain Division. But we never spent much time reminiscing about the war. We didn't talk about the comrades we had left in Europe or the crippled ones who would never make it back to Aspen. We had what we wanted here: Our old army friends and our new Aspen friends, all mixed together in a grand melting pot of skiing.

★ ★ ★ ★ ★

In the early morning we would grab a bite to eat, pack our lunches, and trudge over to the bottom of the new Number 1 lift. The lift towers flowed up the mountain and out of sight near the top of the Corkscrew. The cable had not yet been strung, but the very sight of this shiny new lift made us want to sing out loud as we loaded onto the trucks that would take us up the mountain. Once on top, we worked at tree cutting and cleaning up the slash that remained after the merchantable timber had been hauled down the steep, winding roads to the base.

The days all flowed together. It grew colder, and we watched the skies to the west for the first signs of winter. Finally the cable was spliced, the chairs were hung on the new Heron lift, the cleanup was finished, and we were ready to ski.

Pete and his friend Joe McNealus checking their gear in Idaho Springs prior to heading up to Berthoud Pass for Pete's first postwar race. Though he didn't finish, the race proved to Pete that his war wounds were healing and that he could be competitive again on skis.

deepening November snow that rose to three feet in places. Often we would pack snow from the summit to the base in the morning, have lunch at the bottom, change mitten liners (I would rewrap the bandage brace on my right leg), and then go back to the top in a rattling truck for the afternoon trip down— a total of sixty-four hundred vertical feet of sidestepping. Even the patrolmen with two good legs were pretty beat by the end of the day.

I did all of this with a right knee that had no kneecap and a warped and numb left hand that froze easily. At first, all the sidestepping pulled my leg apart, and the pain was harsh. But gradually I began to feel my upper leg getting stronger, and I knew I would be able to handle ski patrol duties.

But I wanted more: I wanted to race again. I wanted to ski at seventy miles per hour and make perfect turns. To anyone else it may have been a pipe dream, but I thought I could make it happen

by improving my homemade leg brace. The brace I had put together for normal skiing was pretty simple: a six-foot-long, four-inch-wide elastic bandage crisscrossed over my knee, with another elastic support pulled over the whole joint. It offered all I needed for packing, sidestepping, handling a toboggan, and skiing at normal speeds. But it would never be strong enough to resist the forces of a left turn at downhill racing speeds.

My next step was to find a block that I could put behind my knee to keep it from bending beyond forty-five degrees. Bent beyond that point, the ligaments would tear. I pondered this medical puzzle for a while, then ended up putting a full roll of elastic bandage behind my knee, strapping it in place with another bandage and a heavy-duty elastic brace.

At first my left turns were either a series of choppy little step turns or long sweeping curves with about 70 percent of my weight on my good leg and my left ski trailing behind like

Postwar Aspen was a magnet for 10th Mountain Division veterans who'd become hooked on the beauty of the Colorado Rockies. One of them was Stuart Mace, who eventually made a business out of running dogsled trips near Ashcroft.

an outrigger. Still, improvement didn't seem impossible. And after many, many hours of practice with the bizarre new brace, I was turning well and my speed was revving up to downhill velocity. I decided to enter a giant slalom race at Berthoud Pass with my Aspen Ski Club buddies.

At the race I was waiting impatiently at the top when a friend, Joe NcNealus, also of the Aspen Ski Club, broke a binding just minutes from his start time. I offered him my skis. He charged out of the start gate and disappeared down the hill. I figured he'd never get the skis back up in time for my own run and thus I'd be out of the race.

But Joe flagged a car the minute he crossed the finish line, loaded my skis on top, and rode up the highway switchbacks to the top of Berthoud Pass. Only a couple of minutes before my start I saw Joe running toward me, waving the skis. A thirty-second warning sounded just as I finished buckling the straps

around my boots.

"Five, four, three, two, one, *go!*" I launched myself with a mighty shove toward the first gate. The turn to the left was easy. Then I made a right turn—also easy. Next was a sudden fallaway turn to the left—*not* easy. I ended up on my head in deep snow, well beyond the course—a DNF (did not finish) in my first return to postwar racing. Joe had finished third, so I couldn't blame my equipment for the fall.

That turned out to be the worst I did all season. A month later the Rocky Mountain championships were held in Aspen. I won the downhill, the slalom, and the combined. It seemed like a miracle—no, three miracles. Home-field advantage was my only explanation. But it made me believe that I had a chance in the upcoming Roch Cup race. The race was always held in Aspen, on the very difficult Roch Run. And the trophy was the most famous in U.S. ski racing.

I had never felt better. When it was my turn to go, I threw myself down the course. The most dangerous turn on the upper half was at the foot of Zaugg Park, a fallaway right into a narrow mining road. I came successfully blazing out of the road and into a very tricky series of steep turns. I was practically looking through my ski tips into the chimneys of town when I came over the top below Dipsy Doodle. Then I plunged down the celebrated 50 percent grade of the Corkscrew; turned right, left, right; down a steep straight stretch;

Above: There was no better place for a successful ski racer to be in the late Forties than Aspen's Sundeck on a beautiful day. Below: Pete (far right) and his racing buddies (right to left), Gordy Wren, Jerry Hyatt, and George Macomber.

over a road crossing, where I caught lots of air; and then down a field of jarring bumps to the finish.

The hometown folks cheered. I had finished twelve seconds ahead of my closest competitor.

My racing career continued to skyrocket—for a while. Defending the Roch Cup in 1948, I had a squirrelly pair of skis with magnesium bases. They were difficult to control but faster on cold snow than any ski I had ever tried. Unfortunately, the day of the race was warm and sunny, and the snow was soft. Not having been savvy enough to bring backup skis, I practically walked down the course.

Still, I was performing at the top of my sport. I finished third in the giant slalom at the U.S. Nationals in Reno in the spring of 1949, which qualified me for the 1950 U.S. Alpine Ski Team. That was big-time. But not as big as the 1950 FIS World Championships, which were to be held in Aspen the following winter. For the first time, the U.S. would be on the world map of international ski competition. Maybe I could make a good showing. No such luck.

While training with the U.S. team on the ski jump in Sun Valley, Idaho, I fell, tearing chips from my left ankle bone and spraining it severely. Why were Alpine racers ski jumping? Because we always caught lots of air on the Aspen downhill course, and this was thought to be good practice for the downhill. The diagnosis: no skiing for the rest of the season and a plaster ankle cast for at least six weeks.

I tried to make the best of this disaster. Back home in Aspen I found a short child's ski and an army air corps–surplus flight boot. The boot, big and roomy, covered my cast, and I was able to rig it securely to the binding of the short left ski. What do you know? I could ski. My once-

ravaged right leg had gained enough strength to carry my full weight. I rejoiced at this, because when my left ankle healed that leg, too, would be stronger than before and I would be a better skier.

Meanwhile I had my own ideas about what constituted the best medical care. One evening at a cocktail party, I was crutching about, with the ankle cast hanging heavy as a ball and chain. I met a surgeon from Atlanta, and we hit it off. After a few drinks, he agreed with me that it was time to remove the cast. We went to the Aspen hospital, an old Victorian building at the base of Red Mountain. After we buttered up the night nurse, she let the doctor have the saw and whatever else he needed to remove the cast. We then returned to the cocktail crowd unnoticed and continued to drink, to the future health of my limbs and the future prosperity of his practice.

* * * * *

Early in the spring of 1950, I began to suspect that life in Aspen was just too much fun and wasn't leading me where I wanted to go. I had been there for more than four years. The seasons

Acrobatics were an integral part of skiing right from the start. Here Pete attempts a back flip using a small cornice as a launching ramp. Too bad the cornice broke.

THE ULTIMATE SKI OUTFIT

FROM THE 1953 AMERICAN SKI ANNUAL
AND SKIING JOURNAL
BY CHARLES M. DUDLEY

First, let us select the ski, the edges, and the bindings, because they belong in a unit. The ski will be a laminated combination of hickory or other wood. The pieces will be reasonably well matched laterally and vertically so that the strains will be counterbalanced. One ski will match the other and will be straight and free from warps. On each edge of the ski will be a flat-type edge, extending over the tip of the ski.

[Once you've selected your ski], a cable binding will be mounted. It may have a spring ahead, or behind, or be the older Bildstein type heel springs. Don't listen to the experts and get a long thong. You'll go nuts.

Next come the poles. If you want something sensible, get a pair that come to your armpits as you stand on the floor of the ski shop. As for the material, the shafts are usually made of chrome-plated steel, the grip is leather, there is a metal

snow ring with a minimum of leather strap to keep you from sinking too deep in the powder snow, where few people ski today.

The above outfit can be purchased for around $30. There are ways of saving, but cheaper outfits lack respectability and will not give you the fun that a $30 outfit will.

Now let's talk about ski boots. Let's splurge a little here. I'd recommend $35 to get the sort of boot that will give you maximum performance, protection, and durability.

[With regard to clothing] you can go completely "hot dog," or you can get a good conservative outfit that will last you for many years. First, let's talk about trousers. Good all-worsted gabardine is perhaps best. Navy blue is generally accepted year in and year out. A flannel shirt is good—it may be all wool or part wool. Over the shirt have a sweater. Over the sweater a parka or wind-proof jacket is a must. It may be cotton, nylon, or a mixture of synthetics.

The headpiece is a matter of taste, unless you're going to the North Pole. Several years ago it was the ski cap with strings, later "fast" caps, and now the Birger Ruud type jumping toque appears to be the thing. Here's your chance to be daring.

Last but not least you have to have some underwear. If it's warm you may, of course, wear what you usually wear, but it's lots more fun to have red ski underwear that you can display around the ski lodge at night.

blurred gloriously together, and the cycle of work and play repeated itself year after year. Once the winter snow melted, the top of Independence Pass opened to summer traffic, and we began another season of mountain work: new trails to cut, old ones to widen, winter debris to be cleared and burned. There was also lumberjack work, carpentry, truck repairs, and a million other things to do.

For fun we climbed the great rock faces of Pyramid Peak and the Maroon Bells beyond Aspen. We skinny-dipped in mountain lakes that were about two degrees above turning to ice. We rafted on the Roaring Fork River. We played tennis, softball, touch football, and soccer with our European friends. Anything competitive lent itself to a friendly beer bust at the Red Onion bar when the games were over.

With fall came the first golden aspen leaves and the occasional sound of an elk bugling in the distance. The increasingly cold truck rides up the mountain each morning marked the progression from gorgeous autumn radiance to winter frost.

At that time of year the town was almost deserted. Klaus Obermeyer, my roommate for a time in a closet-sized room at the Hotel Jerome, used to come off the mountain and skate on his skis through the empty town. "By the time I reached the Jerome, I would have about ten dogs barking and chasing along behind me," he would later recall.

We had a wonderful crowd in Aspen. The Austrian Friedl Pfeifer and New Englanders Percy Rideout and John Litchfield, all fellow soldiers from the 10th, ran the Aspen Ski School. Steve Knowlton opened the madhouse Golden Horn, where he sold imported Molitor boots in the sports shop upstairs and starred in slapstick floor shows in the cellar restaurant, wearing a bearskin coat, a derby, and sunglasses. Everywhere one turned was something wild and wonderful. The Austrian racer Toni Spiess could ski on one ski while yodeling all the way down Spar Gulch. The actor Gary Cooper played goalie for the weekly broomball games between the ski school and the ski patrol.

Throughout most of my Aspen days, I lived in the same small rustic log cabin across the road from the Red Onion. It was cold in the mornings. But at night, assuming I wasn't participating in an "away game" in a bed elsewhere, my friends and I would gather by the potbelly stove glowing in the corner of the cabin and talk about today's skiing and yesterday's skiing and tomorrow's skiing.

Above: After Pete won the famed Roch Cup in 1947, there were plenty of photographers asking him to pose. Left: After ski patrolling on the mountain all day, Pete waited tables at the Red Onion, owned by fellow 10th Mountain veteran John Litchfield, then walked across the street to his dollar-a-day rental cabin.

Besides the pure joy of daily life in Aspen, there was the mad, colorful world of ski racing, in both winter and spring. Racing was an addictive activity, offering massive doses of glitz, girls, thrills, drama, girls, endless parties, and adoration by the masses, which included girls. In later years, I often thought that if I had won the second Roch Cup in 1948 instead of losing because of my sticky skis, I might have been hooked. I might have committed myself wholly to winning the third Roch downhill and retiring the trophy for good. No doubt I had the genes, the heart, and the ego to spend my life as a racer. But I didn't do it. The dream of building my own ski area was still in place, and I knew there was only one way to make it come true: Work at it. **V**

GOODBYE, ASPEN; HELLO, REALITY

Chamonix et le Mt. Blanc.

Aspen had been my home, my heaven. But I managed to wrench myself away from all that to pursue my dream. In the spring of 1950 I headed for Europe and a formal education at L'École Hôtelière de Lausanne, the Swiss school of hotel management that is still ranked as the best in the world for producing truly superb hoteliers.

The first problem: How was a nearly broke ski racer going to afford such a high-class Continental education? I turned to the GI Bill, which had created a generously funded program for World War II veterans that offered free education of every kind, from automotive repair to molecular biology.

The second problem: All courses at the École were taught in French, and *mon français* was *très minimale*, to say the least. So I took a summer crash course in Berlitz French in Lausanne, Switzerland, then more language studies at the University of Grenoble in France.

After a winter of ski racing and French studies in France, I entered L'École Hôtelière, where for three years I studied the fine art of hotel management, from front office functions to the work of chambermaids. During the summers I worked in

Top: Chamonix, France, where Pete frequently skied, raced, and climbed during his three-year European sojourn in the early 1950s. Bottom: Pete dressed for class at the L'École Hôtelière de Lausanne, where he learned the art of hotel management from the Swiss, the best hoteliers in the world.

luxury hotels such as the Lausanne Palace and the Beau Rivage. I dressed like a true-to-life hotel employee, wearing chef's whites and a big toque in the kitchen, black tie for waiting tables, and a gray wool suit with white shirt and conservative necktie at the reception desk.

Even though I buried myself in the academics of hotel work, I wasn't exactly the class drudge. I was living in the heart of the Alps, with ski areas at every point of the compass. I used my weekends to ski just for the joy of it, or often to race. In the winter of 1951, during my studies in Grenoble, I had raced in the French university championships in Chamonix and finished first in the downhill, slalom, and combined. In the winter of 1952, I entered the Grand Prix de Chamonix, against a world-class field, and finished tenth in the slalom.

The final race of that season was the famous Arlberg Kandahar. All the big-name alpine racers were there, from the great young Norwegian Stein Eriksen to the graceful Austrian Anderl Molterer. I borrowed a pair of downhill skis from James Couttet, a former world champion who owned a sport shop in Chamonix—an extremely fast, very stiff pair of 220-centimeter Dynamics. At first they were great, carrying me at barely controlled speeds toward the final schuss. Then one of those high-octane skis skidded ever so slightly as I hit the last drop, and I lost control in full view of a hundred racing fans watching from the finish line. I flew up into the air; hit the snow and bounced high; hit the snow and bounced again; then hit the snow for the third time and watched as my left ski soared over the crowd into the trees.

The spectators watched this melodramatic fall in shocked silence, sure that I must have sustained some serious injuries as I bounced and rolled. But I rose unhurt. The roar of the spectators echoed off the surrounding Alps: "*Vive l'Americain!*" I pretty much gave up racing that day.

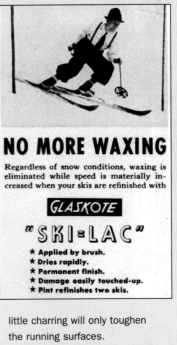

* * * * *

In 1954 I completed my studies, having become an expert in the *service soigné* of Continental hotel management. One of my classmates was Craig Claiborne, who would later revolutionize food and restaurant writing in the *New York Times*. Another fellow student was James Nassikas, whose family owned a restaurant in New Hampshire. Years later, Jim would join with Edgar Stern, an investor from Aspen, to build the elegant and award-winning Stanford Court hotel in San Francisco and Deer Valley Resort in Utah. In 1988 he was elected Hotel Man of the World by his peers.

I next headed back to the relatively coarse world of the Rocky Mountains, which I had come to love more than anywhere in the world. Though my ski-area dream had bloomed in the hard winters of New England, I had decided to transport my vision to Colorado, with its majestic terrain and its magic powder.

The time wasn't yet ripe, however, for my dream to come true. My first job was as the night clerk at the Grand Imperial

Hotel in Silverton, located in the heart of the San Juan Mountains in southwest Colorado. The hotel was neither grand nor did it seem built for an emperor. It had been refurbished in a lurid Gay Nineties decor, and the clientele consisted largely of sightseeing tourists, traveling salesmen, and mountain climbers. Occasionally well-heeled travelers might tip me a quarter for carrying a suitcase.

My hours were from 7 P.M. to 7 A.M. Late at night I escorted drunken cowboys to their rooms, and early in the morning I advised climbers where the best ridges were. I rarely slept. During the day I climbed nearby mountains, conducting a daily search for signs of a potential ski resort. I also hatched an imaginary plot I called "The Great Ski Sting." The plan would be to take options on all the available land in Silverton, bring in European skiers to make tracks down the slide paths above town, and then spread the word around town (in charming, broken English) that the area was perfect for a ski resort. The

Postcard from Europe. Front side (below): Téléférique du Brévent, Chamonix, France. Back side (facing page): ..."Wonderful week at Chamonix. Sunshine every day. I took one of my most spectacular falls and therefore did not place to [sic] well in the downhill..."

78

last step would be to bring in fake planners, surveyors, and architects. At the height of this scam, I would sell the land to the highest bidders and flee to Mexico. It would have made a great movie script.

After a summer in Silverton I returned to Aspen and a job with the Aspen Ski School. I thought Aspen would be the perfect place to meet both potential investors and key staff people for my dream resort—when I finally found it. During that winter of 1954-55 I met a lovely young skier who was spending the winter in Aspen working in a ski shop. Betty Pardee had grown up in Pennsylvania and spent her summer and winter vacations in Lake Placid, New York, with her adventurous father, who was a first-class bobsledder. Her genuine love for the mountains and my own adventurous spirit seemed a good match. We married in the spring of 1955.

My next job involved a real live ski area. To my joy, I landed the job of general manager at the Loveland Pass ski area. It was located on U.S. Highway 6, which was the only major east-west route from Denver to Grand Junction in those days. Loveland Pass—with a base elevation of 10,600 feet and a summit in the clouds at 12,700 feet was the first really developed skiable terrain west of Denver. The annual average snowfall was a humongous 400 inches (in comparison, Aspen averaged 280 inches). Loveland was especially popular with families and older skiers because of its low price (five dollars a day), and because there were no mountain passes to cross when driving up from Denver.

The ski area was a rough operation, even by the relatively rustic standards of the early 1950s. There were some tired rope tows, and the day lodge was an old CCC barracks from the Depression years. As manager I did everything: plow the parking lots, park cars, keep the six rope tows running, and provide all the food, starting with coffee and rolls in the morning, hot dogs and chili at lunch, and late-afternoon cocoa and cookies. The ski patrol was staffed with volunteers from Denver, and the ski school was made up largely of my friends.

I lived with Betty and our one-year-old, Pete Jr., in Georgetown on a steep, twisting two-lane road that became almost impassable in a storm. Many were the times we had to guide a car by walking in front with one hand on the left fender, shepherding the driver through dense snow and high winds past sheer drops, many lacking guardrails or warning signs.

Above: Despite its regal name, the Grand Imperial Hotel in Silverton, Colorado, struck Pete as decidedly rustic compared to the four-star establishments he was used to in the Swiss Alps. But he used his free time to good advantage, exploring the surrounding peaks for a mountain of his own to develop. Facing page: Pete's duties as manager of Loveland Basin ski area during the winter of 1955-56 included everything from supervising the help to shoveling the steps from the parking lot. But he still found time to ski nearly every day—and to perform the occasional geländesprung, as pole-assisted jumps were called in those days. He is following instructor Roy Parker.

One time Betty and I were groping our way at a snail's pace up the west side of Loveland Pass. Little by little our rear wheels began to slip and spin on the snowy road, and the car's rear end swerved dangerously. We needed weight in the back to get some traction. I looked at Betty and said, "Either you or I have to climb in the trunk, dear. Shall we flip a coin?" She replied that there was no need for that and climbed gamely into the trunk, like one of the pioneer women who stood by their men as they struggled to keep moving west. Her 115 pounds were just enough to give our tires grip. Slow as a tortoise, we inched over the top. It was a practical idea, but I never heard the end of it from my friends.

Between Georgetown and the rugged old mining town of Silver Plume, about three miles west, Route 6 was at its most dangerous—a steep, serpentine stretch that included the famous Georgetown Loop, a hair-raising S-turn along sheer drops, which took its toll of several inexpert drivers every win-

ter. Locals had even learned to count on the occasional accident to keep them supplied with certain items. Betty once asked Henry Anderson, the local grocer, if she could buy fresh peaches to can for the winter. Anderson paused, then suggested she wait until the peach trucks came through and see if one tipped over on the Georgetown Loop. When this had happened before, he said, the peaches were bruised, but townspeople had picked them up and found them just fine for canning. And, of course, they were free.

Later that winter the chief maintenance man at Loveland came into my office and asked if I drank booze. I replied, "Yes, now more than ever since I took this job." He asked what kind, and I said Scotch, cognac, and beer. He then said he had plenty of each because he had been behind a liquor truck when it went into a spin on the Loop. Most of the bottles survived the crash unbroken, he said, although the driver did not. He took my order for enough hooch to last until spring. **V**

CHAPTER SEVEN

MONEY TO BUY THE DREAM

In early 1959, Earl and I inducted two new members into the exclusive Transmontane Rod and Gun Club. This made for six members in all. One of the newcomers was Jack Tweedy, a partner in the Denver law firm of Tweedy and Fowler; the other was George Caulkins, president of a Denver oil business. Both were skeptical about committing themselves to my dream, which sometimes seemed to get dimmer as each week went by. Tweedy asked me bluntly, "Peter, is this a hobby or a business?" And Caulkins declared, "My friends suggested I keep my house at Aspen in case Vail doesn't work out." Despite their cynicism, however, both would prove to be absolutely essential to the coming campaign to bring Vail Mountain to life.

* * * * *

By the spring of 1959 Earl and I were finished working for Aspen Highlands. We had learned a lot, and now we were back working exclusively for ourselves—and for Vail. We had accumulated all the complex information we needed about terrain conditions, and we had completed the application for a permit

October 1957. Ute Indians had summered here; rancher John Hanson had grazed cattle here; and Vail Village would rise here. In the center: Golden Peak.

for year-round recreational development on Vail Mountain, to start in 1960. Full of hope and optimism, we filed the request with the Forest Service on May 11, 1959. Less than twenty-four hours later, Paul Hauk gave us our answer: No.

He explained it this way: "We agree that Vail is feasible and has the required potential for another major development in the White River National Forest. However, since we have never given you any encouragement regarding a permit, we are disapproving your application. The reasons are: 1) There is no real public need for the development at this time; 2) We have an obligation to existing area permittees, especially at Aspen, who are entitled to complete their development and be allowed to get into the black before new areas are permitted on this forest."

Reading this far I could hardly swallow. As I read on I

became even more livid. "Our primary obligation," wrote Hauk, "is to Whip Jones at Aspen Highlands. We estimate that he will need until 1965 to show a net profit at his ski area. At that time, we will be happy to reconsider your application. You, of course, have the right to appeal our decision."

We just could not believe the U.S. government would guarantee profits to one private corporation by delaying the development plans of another private corporation. Free competition between two ski areas was being choked off. The whole thing had the vague smell of an antitrust violation, and I said so. We filed an appeal immediately.

The Forest Service rejected it within a week with the same argument: They wanted to give Whip Jones time to profit without competition from a rival Colorado ski area. By now it was August 1959. We had one final appeal. This time we lined up two very powerful, very friendly Colorado congressional representatives— Congressman Wayne Aspinall and Senator Gordon Allott—to argue the Vail side of the conflict. Aspinall stepped up to the plate on August 12 and fired off a smoking letter to Don Clark, head forester in Denver:

I note the action of the Forest Service in denying Vail's application for a special use permit, basing the denial in part on the Forest Service policy that it has an obligation to existing area permittees to help them complete their developments and operate in the black before new areas are permitted to be developed. Don, it seems to be the prevailing philosophy of the Forest Service that it must ... guarantee the financial success of those projects to which it has granted permits or leases—even to the extent of excluding similar projects. I would greatly appreciate your advising me as to the authority whereby this policy has been established. Sincerely, Wayne.

Three weeks later Clark sent a letter to Allott saying that

ALPINE COMPLEX TAKES SHAPE IN THE ROCKIES
FROM SKIING MAGAZINE, OCTOBER 1961

In the West, distances between major resorts have always been measured in hundreds of miles and days of travel. Suddenly this winter the outlines of a major alpine complex are taking shape, all within the confines of a single state. Look at the evidence:

• An alpine resort community, with 6,500-foot double chair lift to open this winter at Breckenridge.
• First stage of a giant complex at Crested Butte, near Gunnison.
• Another complete resort with tramway and double chairlift scheduled for opening this winter on Shadow Mountain, near Grand Lake.
• A $300,000 ski area, called Loveland Valley...adjacent to Loveland Basin and operated by the same management.
• A new double chairlift and resort accomodations set to operate at Guanella Pass, near Georgetown.

In the midst of this phenomenal boom, conservative-minded business leaders in the state are asking if ski area growth is excessive, and if new areas are in for some thin years ahead. They claim some new areas are too remote from popula-

tion centers, and suggest the ski market is not as big as its promoters have claimed.

Forest Service and Colorado Visitors Bureau figures would seem to indicate the risks are less than the possibility of future reward. In five years, skier visits and resulting income to the state have climbed 40 percent, with income estimated at $15 million and skier visits nearing the 500,000 mark at all Colorado areas last year.

Now on the drawing boards are a giant resort near Vail Pass which may rival Aspen and Sun Valley in terrain and facilities, other major areas at Silverton and Telluride in the scenic San Juans, and a scattering of minor areas.

Formerly skeptical, but now solidly behind this winter boom are the railroads, airlines, and bus routes leading into the Rockies.

And as if anxious to emphasize the state's natural claims as an alpine region, three feet of snow fell in the Rockies over Labor Day, prematurely acquainting thousands of summer tourists with the qualities of Colorado winter.

"after considerable negotiations" Vail and the Forest Service had reached a compromise that satisfied both sides.

Indeed we had. The compromise order made no mention of Whip Jones's potential profit or loss. It not only gave us permission to start construction of a year-round recreational development on Vail Mountain in 1961, it also allowed us to begin operation as a bona fide ski area in December 1962. It was signed by the chief of the Forest Service on September 8, 1959.

Looking back some forty years later, I thank my lucky stars

we didn't have to wait until Whip Jones's balance sheets showed black ink. If we had, John Hanson and John Conway might still be kicking tractor tires and spitting at beetles today!

* * * * *

Our grand compromise with the Forest Service was not without a barbed hook or two. Among other things, we were required to have an accumulated total of $1.8 million on hand by December 1961 to cover in advance the cost of trails, lifts, and operating expenses for a year.

Our first step was a baby one. We went to our wealthiest friends in skiing, preferably businessmen or other professionals who had skied in college and still made frequent trips to Europe to enjoy the sport. These people were in the seventy percent tax bracket and could write off good-sized losses with a shrug. They were also experienced in the iffy finances of ski areas. Most had put up some money for New England areas and lost it, but were still willing to put up more money when asked.

Our wealthy friends were eager to help, and by December 1959, three months after the Forest Service compromise order,

we had twenty-one investors in nine different states. Each had bought five thousand dollars worth of stock in the Vail Corporation. This money went to pay some salaries, attorney's fees, and preliminary engineering costs. Most importantly, this money financed the application to the Securities Exchange Commission to issue limited partnership units—one hundred units at ten thousand dollars each—which would give us the first million bucks demanded by the Forest Service to underwrite construction costs and operating expenses.

By now—early in 1960—the Transmontane Rod and Gun Club was quietly dissolved, without a member having directly threatened anything made of fin, feather, or fur. We did use the name Transmontane Company for our official corporation, which was licensed for the early acquisition and disposition of real estate in the Gore Creek Valley. In May 1960 the Transmontane Company bought the Peter E. Katsos ranch, about a mile and a half east of the Hanson Ranch, for $75,000, or $150 an acre, thus adding another five hundred acres to our holdings in the valley.

Between 1958 and 1961 the company's only over-snow vehicle was the Kristi Kat, a plastic bathtub on tracks. It hauled everybody up the mountain, from charter members of the Transmontane Rod and Gun Club to potential investors to inquisitive journalists, including Lowell Thomas. Chances are your driver would have been Earl Eaton.

Bob Fowler, here with his son Robbie, was Vail's first attorney, the man who came up with the name Transmontane Rod and Gun Club. This photo, from the late 1950s, was taken from the north side of the valley looking west. In the valley is the Hanson Ranch and what locals called the "Thick and Thin Sawmill."

At this point we became Vail Associates, Ltd., and we began to operate more like a true business, with a budget to meet and books to balance. We opened a payroll and put Earl and me on it. We also picked an architect to design the village and sought professional advice on sewage, soil, water, roads, and bridges. Moreover, we had to wring some extra cash out of our anemic budget to purchase a herd of fifty cows and a cowboy to care for them. Grazing by livestock was the only way that we could retain a federal grazing permit on the Hanson and Katsos land we owned. If we lost those invaluable grazing privileges there would be no way to get them back, and the value of the land would be seriously reduced.

These were bare-bones days for Vail Associates. In the summer of 1960, someone compiled a list of the corporation's capital assets. Besides land and cattle, the sum total consisted of one jeep, a tin-roofed hut on the summit with an outhouse, and a little red snow vehicle called the Kristi Kat.

* * * * *

At around this time, we got the bad news that someone had applied for a ski-area construction permit for a new develop-

89

ment called Peak 8-10 in Breckenridge. The word was that the Forest Service was leaning toward approving it. The main reason for favoring immediate construction was that the money man behind Peak 8-10 was Bill Rounds, a wealthy heir to a lumber fortune from Wichita, Kansas, who didn't need any help from outside investors. This made our spirits sink, but what sent them sinking the deepest was the ugly and unalterable fact that Breckenridge was thirty miles closer to Denver than Vail.

We protested to the Forest Service that a ski area in Breckenridge meant unfair competition for us. Paul Hauk in particular was unimpressed, however, recalling that during the hearings involving Aspen Highlands we had strongly argued that any and all competition was good for business. He wound up taking sides against Vail in this conflict, too. In January 1961 Hauk and I had a private meeting in Aspen, and he sent the following official report to his superiors:

Seibert appeared quite upset about the Breckenridge competition. I told him he could expect no sympathy from our office due to his 'all for competition' arguments last summer. My personal opinion, as I told Bill Rounds last month, was that the Vail Corporation had no grounds for objecting to Breckenridge since Vail is not an operating or existing area and it does not have a final permit in any sense of the word. I told Seibert that the Forest Service has no guarantee that Vail will ever be built while Rounds has sufficient assets to also develop a few other sites in the Dillon area if he chooses.... Seibert says that his Vail financing 'is coming along' but rumors around Aspen from people who should know are that he is not doing too well and that the Peak 8-10 proposal is causing some to withdraw their support.

Then as now: When early snowfall blankets the Gore Range and the aspens reveal their colors, the view from Mid Vail is enthralling.

Well, I was upset as hell about the Breckenridge encroachment. I was also worried whether we would come close to raising the $1.8 million the Forest Service wanted. So in March 1961 I asked Hauk if he could reduce the cash-on-hand requirement by about $400,000. In response, he wrote a sour memo to his supervisor: "Vail appears to be following the typical ski-area promotion pattern. First, the big 'snow job' with detailed planning, promotion brochures, movies, etc.; then the inevitable paring down when the cash isn't available, compounded by the promoters starting to believe that their 'projected income' for the first five years will take care of operational problems, needed improvements, expansion, etc. etc."

Despite his cynicism, Hauk finally did agree to reduce the total planned capitalization to about $1.6 million—$1.1 million of which would come through the sale of the limited partnership units and roughly $500,000 of which would be in loans guaranteed by the Small Business Administration (SBA) and the First National Bank of Denver. We had to cut out one of our favorite items—the construction of a Swiss-made fifty-passenger jig-back tram that would run from the base to the summit, winter and summer. Instead we put in a shorter four-passenger Bell gondola to Mid Vail. But now we were desperate to get some real cash in hand.

*   *   *   *   *

George Caulkins, a member of the Vail Associates board, had acted as our point man in an early campaign to sell the limited partnership units, which was a common money-raising technique in the oil business. As an incentive for any honest-to-god skiers who might invest, we also threw in four free lifetime lift passes with each partnership.

In George's first foray into fundraising, he visited a number of New York banks and businessmen. He found them all impeccably polite but genuinely puzzled at the idea of investing

Even dreamers have to eat. Left to right: Pete and Betty Seibert, Bob Fowler, and Earl Eaton on the site of Vail Village in 1959.

in a ski resort that didn't yet have a lift or a lodge or a trail in place. The A-list underwriters gave him an undertaker's smile and politely sent George on to the grade-B underwriters, who also murmured regrets and sent him on to the grade-C underwriters, whom no one had ever heard of.

Finally it got through to George and all of us waiting at home that no one in New York banking circles was going to put a dime into a pie-in-the-sky scheme from an alien land called Colorado, which seemed to be located somewhere west of the Hudson River.

So in mid-1960 George and I hit the road together in his sleek silver Porsche, bound for Chicago. We stopped in Fort Collins, Colorado, for coffee, and when we came out of the café a little old lady, dressed in black and sporting a long black cane, was staring at the shining car.

"Say, what is this little thing?" she asked.

"A Porsche," said George.

"Well, it's real cute." She walked around it once, then tapped the hood three times with her cane. She looked at George and winked: "You'll always have good luck, sonny, when you drive a car like this." And she shuffled off.

Was this an omen of coming success? We decided we might as well assume that it was, and with renewed spirits we began the big push to sell Vail to friends, relatives, old school chums,

"...here one day a city shall rise." The Vail Village site in the late summer of 1958. Within four years The Lodge at Vail would come to occupy the spot where the willow bush stands in the right foreground. The line of spruce trees on the left marks Gore Creek.

prize-winning rose garden in Tyler, Texas. Serious skiers came to listen to us everywhere: Milwaukee, Minneapolis, St. Paul, Chicago, Kalamazoo. But not one person bought until early in 1961, when George finally sold our first partnership unit to a cousin of his in Detroit, a man who had never been skiing in his life. With that sale in hand, George immediately got on the phone to people we had already pitched and told them units were selling like crazy. A few people were thus encouraged to buy, but everyone else was reluctant, dubious, and uninterested.

By the summer of 1961 we had sold just thirty-eight of the one hundred units we needed to underwrite our ski area. George went into arm-twisting mode and pleaded desperately with five wealthy Vail Associates board members. If each one would promise to underwrite five partnerships (at ten thousand dollars a piece), George would underwrite ten of them. They agreed, and George put up his promised amount. That put us near our goal.

Finally, while driving through Texas on a sweltering August day, George and I came up with a dazzling new twist on our partnerships that brought in—and brought back—many new people as well as dozens of those who had turned us down. As I mentioned, we had already promised four lifetime passes with every partnership unit. But now we realized that we could add something even more valuable to each investor: a piece of land for a homesite in Vail Village. Price: a meager five hundred bucks. (Price today: well in excess of one million dollars.)

This unprecedented idea became the deal clincher for many, many investors. And it put us over the top. As George said, "People in Texas and other places, too, had no idea what the value of lift passes might be worth, but they had no doubt about

country club pals, army buddies, and others. As George would tell someone much later on: "I can't tell you how many thousands of miles we covered. It wasn't like raising money for oil wells. Putting together a ski area as a money-raising proposition had never been done before. If we hadn't had a lot of good friends who came in on a questionable investment based on friendship, we wouldn't have been able to do it."

True enough. I think it helped that we always told potential investors up front that they had little chance of ever getting a return on their money. That kind of honesty appealed to a lot of people—don't ask me why.

Our road show went on for weeks. One of the centerpieces of our sales talk was a silent, fifteen-minute black-and-white movie about skiing at Vail. We went all over the Midwest, the Northeast, and the Southwest, always talking and showing that film. We made sales pitches in penthouses, suburban bungalows, motel rooms, yacht clubs, and country clubs; at the Mayo Clinic in Minnesota, on a tugboat in Newport, Rhode Island; and in a the value of land."

Everything had finally come together. We had the first million-plus dollars, and the other five hundred thousand was covered by the SBA and by Denver bank loans. We threw a party to declare our victory, and the next day, December 29, 1961, the *The Denver Post* ran the headline: HUGE NEW SKI AREA IN WORKS. The story that followed could only be called ecstatic: "Colorado skiing took another giant jump forward Thursday with the news the state is getting still another ski area—this one to be the largest in the U.S. The Vail area, to be built on the west side of Vail Pass, sounds like a honey. It will have a large gondola lift, a pair of mile-long chairs, a 3,000-foot descent, wide-open bowls, an alpine village—the works!"

Ah, yes. The works!

On March 1, 1962—just sixteen days short of five years from the day Earl Eaton and I climbed the no-name mountain—I received and signed the final Forest Service construction permits as "Peter W. Seibert. General Partner for Vail Associates, Ltd." I was taking responsibility for 6,470 acres of land—seven square miles of spectacular skiing terrain. My dream now included a 9,500-foot gondola; two chair lifts, each a mile long; a 1,000-foot beginners lift; a village.... All I could think was that I had come a long, long way from those daily milk runs to the farm below the hill in Sharon, Massachusetts. **V**⚬

Gore Creek, the epicenter of Vail Valley and the focal point of village life in the summertime. The creek starts high above in the Gore Range, joins the Eagle River after leaving the valley, then joins the Colorado River farther west at Dotsero. Despite the proximity of Vail Village today, the trout fishing in the creek is still remarkably good.

CHAPTER EIGHT

BUILDING THE DREAM

At the same time the commercial center of the village was taking shape along Bridge Street, the pioneers were building themselves homes nearby.

★ ★ ★ ★ ★

Summer finally came, the mountains dried out, and the oceans of mud were replaced by billowing clouds of dust roiled up by trucks and dozers. It rose above the treetops in places, casting a brownish pall over the summer-green valley.

The housing shortage that had plagued us earlier had been solved by bringing in rows and rows of trailers, which some two hundred of our workers occupied. For them, the work was the thing, and whether nature served up mud, dust, or black flies, they charged along, keeping us ahead of schedule and producing some kind of new miracle of construction every day. June Simonton reported in her book, *Vail, Story of a Colorado Mountain Valley*:

> As the summer of 1962 rolled along, a steady stream of suppliers chugged over the narrow Vail Pass road, and the ripsaw screech and hammer blow of construction in the great sheep pasture rose to fever pitch. Seibert, the visionary, served as corporate chief, construction manager and consummate cheerleader. Every hour of every day another decision had to be made. Seibert made them quickly.

Indeed, I did—very quickly. Nothing could be considered for very long, and if something had to go someplace that we hadn't planned it for, we just put it there. There was no time for studies or second thoughts about anything.

★ ★ ★ ★ ★

Two basic construction jobs were going on at the same time: the village along the one-mile strip at the base of the mountain and the clearing of liftlines, construction roads, and ski trails up to the summit and into the Back Bowls.

No ski area can thrive on skiing alone; a commercially viable village at its base is a must. Three of the major areas in Colorado—Aspen, Telluride, and Breckenridge—originally were colorful old mining towns full of character and Victorian architecture. But Vail Village grew out of raw wilderness and bare grazing land. I knew from the start I wanted a town that contained pieces of several ski resorts in the Alps: St. Anton and Kitzbühel in Austria; Méribel, France; and Zermatt, Switzerland, the classic Swiss village at the bottom of the Matterhorn. I had visited Zermatt several times and admired it so much that I eventually memorized the town blueprints, with the idea of bringing Zermatt to Colorado. I even measured the length and width of its streets and took photos of buildings that were especially appealing.

Zermatt has no cars, and the only way to get there then was by train through the mountains. During one visit I followed a crowd of skier down a narrow street away from the train station. Soon I noticed that many brightly lit shops had sprung up along this seemingly out-of-the-way street. Why? I turned a corner, and there was a new ski lift on the edge of the village. The idea seemed logical: Lead skiers past tempting shops to bring them to the ski lift. I replicated this concept in Vail Village, designing Bridge Street so that it would curve neatly past a large assortment of shops, bars, and restaurants on the way to the mountain lifts. And we decided to allow no cars in the town. The parking lot was across Gore Creek, between Highway 6 and the bridge over the creek, which later became the covered bridge.

All of this began in that waterlogged spring of 1962, when the village pioneers began to wander into this primitive outpost to seek their fortunes and carve a new hometown out of rocks and thin air. There were maybe seventy-five permanent residents, and life was harsh at times. Our "great communicator," Bob Parker, described it this way: "As with any pioneer community, the streets were unpaved, so there was a lot of mud, a lot of dust, and a lot of dogs. Walking along Bridge Street, you'd see horses hitched to the street light posts. In summer from about mid to late June, sheepherders would drive their sheep through the middle of town and up the road on the other side, to spend the summer on the mountain. One time, a dog chased a sheep through a ground floor apartment window. The owner came home to find a live sheep, a broken window, and sheep's blood all over her new white carpet."

* * * * *

As Vail was being built, we were always balancing on the brink of failure, trying to be ready for any surprise disaster that might arrive and never being able to guess how bad the next news might be. In

OTHER MEN'S MEMORIES: BOB PARKER

As unlikely as it may seem for a place founded in 1962, Vail had all the elements of Colorado's gold and silver boomtowns of the Nineteenth century. First, there was its mineral wealth. No, not silver or gold or copper or lead. Just plain H_2O in the form of snow, the raison d'être of the resort and the source of the town's wealth. White gold, some of us called it.

Then there were its other natural resources. Lots of limestone-rich spring and river water, once used to make Gore Creek's version of moonshine whiskey. Plentiful sunshine. Fabulous scenery. Mountain ridges that sheltered the valley from the worst of winter winds. Mountain slopes both gentle and steep and the unique, never-to-be-forgotten Back Bowls. And Charlie Vail's Highway 6 snaking down the valley, providing just enough access for the food, liquor, and building materials needed to put up a future world-class resort.

Everyday conditions in the Vail Valley were quintessentially pioneer. Knee-deep mud. Drought. Forest and grass fires. House fires. Landslides. An eight-party phone system that was never available in a real emergency. Suppliers who would never take your checks, because they'd never heard of Vail.

Drunks and crazies off the highway. Looky-loos who stopped in August to ask, "Where's the skiing?" No schools, so the pioneers created one. No television, so people actually talked to one another.

And then there were the pioneers themselves, a group as eerily diverse as their earlier counterparts in the Colorado mining days. People from England, Australia, Switzerland, and Austria. A Michigan banker turned restaurateur. A millionaire oilman's son working as a bartender. A Vermont radio executive running a gift shop and building a covered bridge to remind him of home. A Colorado businessman publishing the town's first newspaper. A rich kid from Minneapolis sleeping in a snowbank so he could follow his dream of building a ski lodge in the Rockies.

Everyone did everything. All the men were volunteer firemen. All the women hauled hoses and made sandwiches for the firefighters. All the kids ski raced in winter and rode horseback in summer. When someone was hurt, someone else would drive him or her to the nearest clinic ten miles away. The ski bums sneaked out in the autumn to kill a deer or elk so they'd have meat for the winter.

Pioneers in 1962? Yes, it sounds crazy. But don't tell early Vailites they weren't pioneers. You had to have been there, in the mud and cold, fighting fires, inventing ways of surmounting problems, helping your neighbors, and always waiting, as with the old pioneers, for that first strike, for the first snows of winter. If that wasn't pioneering, then I don't know what is.

CHAPTER NINE

LET IT SNOW

Opening day at Vail was not auspicious. The lifts were free, yet the locals riding the gondola just for the view outnumbered the actual skiers. As Rod Slifer would say later, we were so busy putting the finishing touches on everything that "there was no time to stop and congratulate each other." He also said the day made so little impression on him that he didn't even remember the exact date.

I remember the date—December 15, 1962—but it certainly wasn't a day of unmitigated triumph. As June Simonton wrote in her history of Vail, "So Vail began with dust in its streets and the snow at its crest only ankle deep. Peter Seibert, who made all the right moves on the long road from dream to reality, had the last vital decision taken out of his hands. He could not make it snow." In fact, there was so little early-season snow that I had been able to drive my 1958 Volvo sedan to the summit on December 6.

Above: December 12, 1962. Three days before the grand opening. A spanking new Bell gondola to carry skiers to Mid Vail. Great new trails to ski. But no snow. In fact, there wouldn't be significant snow until just before Christmas. Below: When early snowfall was scarce at the start of the second season, Indians from the Southern Ute tribe were invited to provide a snow dance. It worked.

* * * * *

Bob Parker had arranged for a U.S. Olympic team training camp a week after the official opening. It still hadn't snowed much, and the team formed bucket brigades to bring snow out of the woods and pack it on their racecourses. Parker had also made sure the press would be on hand to cover the Olympians and report on the new mountain.

The mountain had already received some national publicity. A story in *Sports Illustrated* a few months before we opened quoted University of Denver ski coach Willy Schaeffler as saying Vail

would never be a success because the mountain was too flat, with not enough steep runs for your average expert skier. Some of our board members were appalled. I told them, "You guys wait. This will be the best thing that ever happened to us."

Our phones rang off the hook. Negative though it seemed, that report sounded just right to hundreds of non-expert skiers who had been frightened by some of the steep and icy runs at Alta, Sun Valley, and Aspen. Everyone was making reservations at Vail for its "comfortable" skiing.

That didn't mean we were overwhelmed with skiers, however. We had only three lifts that first winter: the gondola from the village; one chairlift out of Mid Vail; and another chair out of the Back Bowls. The slopes were nearly empty, and sometimes we could still find untracked powder on the mountain three days after a big dump. On weekdays there were so few customers that the eight ski instructors often had no one to teach. The worst day of all for income came in January when I counted twelve skiers who paid five dollars each. On another day, later in the season, I took a head-count of everyone on the mountain: fifty employees and thirty-eight paying guests, scattered over seven square miles.

Our early capacity was 1,500 skiers on the mountain. We had reached that number only six times by the late winter of 1964. Then on the Saturday before Easter that year, a brilliant day with a dazzling blan-

Above: Originally, Mid Vail was a modest, flat-roofed building with an expansive sundeck. The signature second story with its big windows was added later. Below: March 1963. How many 1962 Chevrolet Corvairs can you spot in the parking lot?

demanded that their money for lift tickets, meals, and rooms be refunded immediately, and it was. I signed the requisition for the cash on the spot. And the board voted yes to the three new lifts.

* * * * *

Of course, snow is always a variable in the ski business. Ski-area operators are just as dependent on the weather as any orange grower fighting frost in Florida. Nowadays, snowmaking has taken a certain amount of the anxiety out of the business. But we would have given our eyeteeth to have had just one snowmaking machine in the first years that Vail was open. Snowfall the first season had started out weak but built nicely. The second season (1963–64), however, we had wall-to-wall blue skies throughout the fall.

We were worried we'd get a reputation for never having early snow. One day around Thanksgiving a woman who worked in Vail Blanche, our first ski shop, suggested to Bob Parker that the Ute Indians might perform a dance for us that would stimulate a change in the weather. The idea was for

ket of new snow, crowds rushed to our mountain like nothing we had ever seen or dreamed of before. No fewer than 1,976 people paid to ski, and to our disbelief, they were forced to wait to board the gondola for up to twenty minutes!

It was a resounding embarrassment, but as had already happened in Vail's brief history, a seemingly negative episode became a positive one for us. On that same sunny Saturday I was in a meeting with our board of directors and our bankers, discussing whether or not we had enough capital to build three new chairlifts the following summer. The mood was skeptical, and the pending vote looked to be a nay.

Just then word came from the mountain: Four college boys on their spring break had tired of the "long" lines and decided to drive on to Aspen. They had

O PIONEERS: SOME OF THE EARLY RESIDENTS

John Amato and Vince Daminico from Denver put up our first combination delicatessen, coffeehouse, and liquor store—blessed additions if ever there were any.

Larry Burdick, a friend of then Congressman Gerald Ford of Kalamazoo, Michigan, built the Red Lion restaurant.

Charlie Gersbach, a one-time Denver travel agent, was the first manager of the Vail Village Inn.

Dave and Renee Gorsuch drove up from their shops in Gunnison and Crested Butte, liked what they saw, and opened ski, sporting goods, and clothing stores in the new Clock Tower built by John and Lorrie McBridge.

The Austrian ski racer Pepi Gramshammer, along with his radiant wife Sheika, started out as Vail's sponsored pro racer and stayed on to buy a prime corner lot close to the Covered Bridge to build his lodge, restaurant, and sport shop.

Sigfried Faller, Jr., formerly manager of silver-spoon hotels in Europe, was the first manager of The Lodge at Vail.

Dick and Blanche Hauserman built Vail Blanche, a ski shop and rental operation, at the base of the gondola.

On Bridge Street Ottie Keuhn from Milwaukee built the first pharmacy and trinket shop, while Ted and Nancy Kindel came to ski the place, loved it, and stayed to build the Christiana Lodge. Later Ted was Vail's first mayor.

Manfred Schoeber, a German tourist, left his skis and gear next to Route 6 and walked into the construction site to ask if there was a job. He wound up building a sport shop with several apartments on Bridge Street.

Morrie Shepard, my old childhood friend from Sharon, Massachusetts, agreed to leave the directorship of the Aspen Ski School and come to run the school in Vail. He brought his pal Rod Slifer. With no ski school underway yet, the two of them got deeply involved in construction jobs. Morrie worked on gondola construction and Rod was sort of a clerk of the works who knew where everything was and later became our corporate real estate man.

them to do a tribal dance to bring snow. We contacted a man named Eddie Box, who handled ceremonial dances for the Bear Clan. Parker asked him if they performed snow dances and was told, no, only rain dances. Could Eddie Box make an exception this time? Eddie said that only Minnie Cloud, an ancient member of the Cloud Clan, had good enough contacts with the weather gods to answer that question. So Minnie checked with the gods and said a snow dance would be okay.

Parker then alerted the press, explaining, "The scheduled dance is actually a rain dance. However, tribe officials have given approval to a temporary change of nomenclature, and the dance will be called a snow dance this one time only. Because of

temperatures at Vail, we are very hopeful that the dance will produce snow rather than rain. Rain, of course, would be disastrous, but we're willing to take that chance."

About a half-dozen Utes arrived in Vail Village on December 9. The entire group, including Eddie Box, who proved to be a short, powerful fellow, and Minnie Cloud, a tiny but majestic woman, emerged from his Cadillac. The whole party of Utes danced that afternoon at the lodge; the skies grew dark, and an icy wind blew. There was no snow, though, and the next day the sun blazed down from a perfect blue sky.

The Utes and some Vail officials then took the gondola up and joined an excited crowd of skiers at Mid-Vail. Minnie Cloud stretched her wrinkled hands to the sky and spoke in her own tongue to the weather gods. Eddie Box urged us and the gathered skiers to join in the dance. We all did.

The Utes left the next day in brilliant sunshine. Three days later, on December 14, Parker called Eddie Box and mentioned that it was still sunny at Vail. The Ute replied that Minnie Cloud said she could feel a snowstorm coming. Two days later, clouds rolled in, dense and gray, and on December 17 a blizzard slammed us. There was plenty of snow until late April. The only sour note in the whole episode came from a fundamentalist church in eastern Colorado, which denounced us for using "heathen tactics" to make it snow.

Of course, the obsession with snow is ever present in the ski business, but in the 1960s and early 1970s resort operators were even more concerned because the ski boom was exploding all around us. Every successive year of Vail's first decade we made more money from more skiers than before. In the U.S. the number of skiers leaped from 1,584,250 in 1960 to 2,448,000 in 1964. Colorado destination resorts led the way in this quantum growth: In 1964, 393,196 visitors came to resorts like ours; in 1968 there were 749,719. Vail jumped from 55,000 in 1962–63 to 546,000 in 1971–72. If it didn't snow early in the season—definitely before Thanksgiving—these armies of

Marketing effort, summer of 1963. Hoping to induce motorists to stop and ride the gondola to Mid Vail and maybe buy a lunch or two, Vail Associates hung a gondola car from a light pole out by Route 6 and put a couple of dummies in it. Unfortunately, the dummies couldn't wave at the passing motorists to flag them down.

eager skiers and the dollars they represented would shrink drastically. So we were always alert to new techniques for bringing the white stuff down as early as possible.

Among the most persistent of the weather-fixers was a loquacious fellow named Neal Bosco, who habitually contacted ski resorts in the late fall and guaranteed that he could make it snow by Thanksgiving. He had the air of a mad scientist, but we were desperate men if snow hadn't fallen in November.

We once hired Bosco to fly over the ski area just as a snowstorm seemed to be gathering over the Gore Range. He had loaded a couple hundred pounds of silver iodide into the aircraft, along with what he would only refer to as his "secret ingredient." He intended to fly into the eye of the storm and throw buckets of the silver iodide mixed with the secret ingredient into the clouds to increase snowfall. Did it work? I recollect we had a dump of about a half-inch of snow that smelled vaguely like battery acid.

Usually Bosco worked on the ground, however, relying on high-firing flares to spray particles of silver iodide into the air. It had to be snowing, or at least threatening to snow, before he was ready to begin. He would then phone us to help him set up spotlights and arrange the flares. If all went well, you could expect a 10 to 15 percent increase in snowfall, possibly even more. A group of ski areas, including Vail, Arapahoe Basin, and Breckenridge hired Bosco one dry December for a month of cloud seeding. According to our agreement, if the snowfall exceeded a certain depth by twelve or more inches he would get a bonus. When I asked Larry Jump of Arapahoe Basin where

we should measure the snowfall for the bonus, he chuckled: "On the hood of a car with the engine running."

Neal Bosco was nothing if not versatile. On another occasion he called me from Albuquerque and asked what would happen if a ski area got too much snow. I said that was practically impossible: Snow was snow, and when it fell it was great for the ski business, no matter what. But Bosco had been thinking along different lines. He reminded me that he was in northern New Mexico and said that a big blizzard seemed to be building there. He had a proposition: If I would wire him five hundred dollars, he believed he could turn the storm toward Aspen.

I was puzzled. Toward Aspen? Why?

He explained that if this storm dumped a huge amount of snow on Aspen, the ski area would be forced to close down because of the threat of avalanches. Wouldn't shutting down Aspen be worth five hundred dollars to Vail?

I said no, it wasn't worth that, plus it wasn't worth the risk of getting caught in history's first criminal assault by blizzard. Moreover, I was about 90 percent certain that he had called D.R.C. Brown, president of Aspen, and made him a similar proposal with Vail as the victim.

Several ensuing years of good pre-Thanksgiving snowstorms passed through Colorado, and Neal Bosco never appeared again, which was too bad. He had provided a lot of laughs, and he had never once used a "heathen tactic," as far as I know. **V**

CHAPTER TEN

THE GLORY YEARS: 1963–1976

For the most part snowfall was ample and consistent during Vail's glory years, giving powder skiers the conditions they craved in the Back Bowls.

I don't think there has ever been a period in my life more filled with good luck, good news, and all-around good vibrations than the first decade or so of Vail's existence. Those were the glory years. They raced past like a mad river roaring down a great canyon, and every morning I awoke before dawn, so excited by the prospect of facing another set of unknown rapids that I couldn't sleep.

I remember standing on my skis at the summit one morning in the winter of 1968. I had gone up with some members of the ski patrol, who were going to test a new batch of avalanche charges. It was just getting light. The boys on the patrol headed toward the Back Bowls in fresh powder, and for a moment I was alone. I looked up at the waning stars and thought of the day in 1957 when I had brought my dreams up here and changed my life forever, to say nothing of the lives of thousands of other people who worked or played or prospered because of Vail. The no-name mountain had turned into the most successful ski

resort in North America, and I was on the pinnacle of success. But as with everything in those busy, productive years, I had no time to savor the moment. The patrolmen were calling "Pete! Pete!" and I charged after them through the powder.

* * * * *

There were lots of milestones that marked our success. In the third season, 1965–66, we started racking up more skier days than any of our Colorado competitors. By our fifth year we were pulling in 250 percent of our initial projections. An article in SKI Magazine in 1969 called Vail one of the "super-resorts of American skiing." The next year SKIING Magazine wrote: "Vail has everything a vacationing skier could want."

Even business writers were paying attention to Vail. In

December 1963, the business editor of *The Denver Post,* Willard Haselbush, wrote:

> Two years ago this new Colorado boom town was a sheep pasture. Now it has $8,480,000 worth of new construction—homes, apartments, restaurants, lodges, nightclubs, shops, and ski facilities—with a minimum of $3 million in construction already set for 1964. Construction in Vail Village began just nineteen months ago. Since then fifty private homes have been built, many in the $100,000 bracket, and one that cost $500,000 without landscaping and furnishings.

Yes, we were in boom times right from the start, and it was not just because of the sale of individual houses. In large part our real-estate success was due to a Colorado law passed in 1963 that allowed condominium ownership without ownership of the land. This fueled the condominium boom, opening up space that could be purchased for one-fourth the price of a house. Because the land in our narrow valley was limited, prices rose astronomically throughout the Sixties, and a condo in Vail soon became a national status symbol. As Rod Slifer told June Simonton when she was researching her history of Vail, "It was incredible in those years. There was no negotiation on price. Bang! If one guy didn't take it, the next guy would."

* * * * *

The resort was growing so quickly that by the mid 1960s it was clear that Vail Associates couldn't keep paying for municipal needs, such as roads, sewers, new schools, or someone to round up stray dogs. For years I had been the unofficial dogcatcher, operating sans salary or budget. When stray dogs appeared in town, I simply locked them up and charged their owners for room and board. Obviously, this couldn't continue forever.

So Vail Associates hired a city manager, Blake Lynch, to take the necessary steps to form an incorporated town. Our goal was to create a partnership with the community based on goodwill and common interests, a relationship that would stand the test of time. I think we have succeeded wonderfully. Compared to some other Colorado resorts, where the resort company and the elected town officials are often at loggerheads, the relationship in Vail has mostly been one of cooperation and mutual respect.

In 1966 the Town of Vail came into being, with a mayor and a town council. Our first mayor was Ted Kindel, who had taken a leadership role in the community almost as soon as he arrived. He and his wife, Nancy, built one of the earliest lodges, and he served as both fire chief and on the board of the first school.

The second mayor was John Dobson, who served from 1966 to 1976. When he and his wife, Cissy, arrived in Vail in the early Sixties, they had opened a general store on Bridge Street. It was

BEHIND THE TRAIL NAME: FOREVER

The winter before Vail opened, Pete and I had begun talking to Austrian racer Pepi Gramshammer about coming to Vail from Sun Valley. During a professional ski race at Loveland Basin, we invited him to come the next day and take a look at Vail Mountain. Transported by Kristi Kat to the summit, Pepi loved everything about the place. After a lunch at our summit cabin, we skied around the summit until reaching the long, open slope on the southwest side. The snow was perfect spring corn, so Pepi, Morrie Shepard, and Pete launched themselves down the slope in huge sweeping christies. Earl Eaton and I, knowing there

was no way out of there but on foot, stayed behind with the cat. When the tired but elated trio finally trudged up to us, Pepi was ecstatic. "By *Gott*," he exclaimed. "*Dot's* a super slope!" Then, catching his breath, he admitted, "but it takes *foreffer* to climb out!"—Bob Parker

Left: For the dedication of the new Lionshead gondola in 1969, Vail Associates hired a lion named Simba to add some majesty to the proceedings. Above: Pete Seibert, lion tamer for a day.

THE NAKED MAN

One quiet winter morning during one of Vail's first years, a few early risers were trudging up Bridge Street when the silence was shattered by angry cries. Down the street came a totally naked man, followed by a clearly furious, fully dressed citizen wielding a small axe. Two of the early risers, ski patrolmen on their way to the gondola, stopped the angry citizen and gingerly relieved him of his axe. Meanwhile, running barefoot down the icy street as if on red-hot coals, the naked one rounded the corner into Gore Creek Drive and disappeared into a row of condominiums under construction.

Since there was no official police presence available that early in the morning, and since the outraged axe wielder had calmed down enough to return to his dwelling, no further action was taken to find the mysterious and undoubtedly chilblained gentleman *sans-culottes*. But the local rumor mills soon identified the runner as a well-known lady's man, who had been surprised *in flagrante* with the wife of the axe wielder, who had returned unexpectedly from out of town. Nothing better depicts the civilized and forgiving nature of early Vail society than the fact that a few weeks later the cuckold and cuckolder were seen at a local bar having a friendly drink together!—Bob Parker

* * * * *

In the Sixites it was common for ski resorts to hire famous ex-racers to run the ski school. Our choice was Roger Staub, a Swiss skier who had won the gold medal in giant slalom at the 1960 Winter Olympics. A great athlete as well as a charismatic host at après-ski parties, Staub became a Vail icon, appearing in thousands of photographs and dozens of films wearing his signature white hat. He and fellow Swiss skier Art Furrer, plus American freestyle pioneer Tom LeRoi, did flips in Vail's early promotional films, setting the stage for the birth of freestyle skiing in the 1970s. Vail went on to host many of those early freestyle events, further bolstering our image as a "happening" place.

* * * * *

In 1969 we opened the Lionshead section of the mountain, as well as the village at its base, both named after a rock outcropping above the neighboring town of Minturn. We built a second gondola, cut new cruising trails on the front side—Simba, Bwana, and Born Free—and opened Game Creek Bowl on the back side of the mountain. That gave us a total of seven chairlifts, two gondolas, four beginners' lifts, twenty-eight restaurants, forty-five hundred beds, and a ski school with seventy instructors—and an all-day lift ticket was only eight dollars. For the dedication of Lionshead, Bob Parker had the brilliant idea of importing a real lion. An animal named Simba arrived, accompanied by a suspiciously nervous trainer. Simba climbed the steps leading to the new lower gondola terminal. Just as he entered the door, Simba brushed against a loose wire in a string of Christmas bulbs and received an electrical shock. He leaped into the building, yanking the trainer along on his chain leash, and made several lunges at people before settling down.

Parker wanted me to pose for pictures in a gondola car with Simba, and I agreed reluctantly. The lion got in with me, then made a guttural sound in his throat. I interpreted it as a threatening growl and jumped out. Other people within earshot claimed it was only a gentle belch, but I'll stick with my interpretation. After all, I was the one with my arm around his neck.

★ ★ ★ ★ ★

Of course, not everything happened the way we wanted it to. In the late 1960s the face of the valley changed forever when the state condemned 110 acres of Vail Associates property and began to transform quaint, twisting U.S. Highway 6 into high-speed, high-capacity Interstate 70. I told Charlie Shumate, director of the state highway department, that he could put his new interstate highway in some other valley—I didn't want it. After all, if Aspen didn't suffer from being at the end of a circuitous road, neither would Vail. But Charlie saw his highway as a blessing for any community it went through, and, of course, we really had no choice in the matter. We did manage to get more cash from the state for our 110 acres than was originally offered, but we had to go to court to do it. The initial offer had been for $298,000; after a lengthy court case we settled for about $850,000. But I still wish I-70 had been built somewhere else.

With the formation of the Town of Vail in the Sixties, an on going effort was begun to beautify public spaces, such as this open area between the parking structure and the Covered Bridge.

★ ★ ★ ★ ★

We always had wonderful press coverage in those early years, due in large part to the fact that Bob Parker was extremely well liked by journalists. In 1964 *Sports Illustrated*'s cosmopolitan ski editor, Fred Smith, delivered a hugely enthusiastic report:

> Today, in the vicinity of Gore Creek, where not even a mining shack existed before, a dozen saunas

now flourish. Smoke escapes the chimneys of seventy-two houses, ranging from a ski chateau with walls painted in trompe l'oeil to simple, rustic cottages. Liquor stores are stocked with Western-sized bottles of Beefeater and with Pommard and muscatels that would do a Madison Avenue vintner proud. *Blanquette de veau* is served in a downstairs *boîte* called La Cave where University of Colorado students in jeans dance a Wild West version of the Watusi and Long Island ladies in long skirts do genteel versions of the frug.

The chalets, the saunas, the Pommard and the frug are the appurtenances of ski areas around the world.

But never in the history of U.S. skiing have they all come so quickly; never has a bare mountain leaped in such a short time into the four-star category of ski resorts.

* * * * *

As an ex-ski racer, the most magical times for me were when the world's best racers came to town. We had assumed from the start that big-time racing would be an integral element of our image, and as a result no American resort emphasized it as consistently as we did. Beginning in 1964, when the U.S. stars were Jimmie Heuga and Billy Kidd, we scheduled an event nearly every year.

I found many lifelong friends among

In the Sixties, Vail was one of the few American resorts to regularly stage international ski races. When Jean-Claude Killy (top, right) first came to Vail, he was "just another French hot dog," as SKIING Magazine called him. His Olympic medals and world fame were still years away. But by March 1967 Killy was on a roll, winning four consecutive races on four consecutive days at Vail.

these great racers. For example, Karl Schranz, the rugged Austrian, became a respected friend—but not until after the Vail ski patrol pulled him off the hill and brought him to my office because he had jumped out of Chairlift 1. The giant slalom course was directly under the lift, and Karl didn't see any reason why he should have to wait until the chair reached the top to get a closer look. I gave him a short, stern lecture. Karl barked back, and I snarled that I would see that he was disbarred from all races unless he abided by Vail's safety regulations. Angrily, he agreed. Now, years later, we laugh about that confrontation.

Karl was a magnificent skier with miraculous longevity: He won his first world-class downhill in 1959, when he was nineteen, and his nineteenth in 1973, when he was thirty-three. When he began racing, downhill racers wore wooden skis and averaged less than fifty miles per hour. When he finally retired, skis were made of metal or fiberglass, and racers hit speeds of more than eighty miles per hour.

Then there was the coach of the French women's team, Honoré Bonnet, a crafty fellow who would do anything to win. Once at Vail he brought his entire giant slalom team to the start gate late, claiming they had overslept—all eight racers and several coaches. Could that be? No. The weather had changed drastically in the hour before the race, and Bonnet had sent them en masse to the wax room to change wax. The French women scored better than anyone in the race, and when I was handing out the prizes later in the day, I called Bonnet to the platform and gave him a large alarm clock so his team wouldn't "oversleep" again.

During one of our early races, some members of the French ski team drove to Glenwood Springs, sixty miles west, and bought cowboy hats and a pistol. On the way back, they used the pistol to take pot shots at geese on the Colorado River and got stopped by an irate state patrolman. It took some smooth talking from Vail Associates to straighten out the mess.

Hi jinks aside, the French skiers were the cream of the crop in those years, athletically and socially. No one was better in both areas than Jean-Claude Killy, who went on to win three gold medals at the 1968 Winter Olympics. He was the epitome of Alpine ski racing—the crown prince of his sport—as well

BEHIND THE TRAIL NAME: LOST BOY

During Vail's second winter, a distressed relative called the office to report that her nephew, a 12-year-old boy, who had been skiing alone, had failed to show up at the end of the day. We notified the patrolman on the mountaintop by phone, who then begin organizing the first, and probably the biggest, patrol and volunteer search in Vail's history. There were not nearly enough patrolmen for the task, so they dragooned good skiers, instructors, businessmen, bartenders, and company officers, and assembled us all on the summit. A half-dozen groups, each one led by a patrolman, swept the mountain. Nothing of the lost boy was found during a long, frustrating night. The next day, while most of the volunteers were back at work, several patrolmen and ski bums were descending a ridge south of what became Game Creek Bowl in heavy spring snow when they came upon a tired but healthy kid walking up the ridge, dragging his skis. Having become lost after slipping under an out-of-bounds rope, he had remembered his Boy Scout training, made a bed of spruce boughs, and spent a cold but otherwise uneventful night. One search team had passed close by and called his name, but he must have been asleep. When Game Creek Bowl was opened a few years later, only one name fit the broad trail on that ridge.—Bob Parker

as a young man of dignity, grace, and humor—always humor. I remember skiing the Back Bowls with Jean-Claude and his teammate Léo Lacroix. Killy was complaining about the way his left ski felt in the turns. We stopped at the top of Ricky's Ridge in Sundown Bowl, and Killy asked if anyone had a nickel. I did and gave it to him. He promptly loosened his bindings, slid the nickel under the sole of his left boot, fastened the bindings, and proceeded to do the most magnificent set of powder turns I had ever seen. "See what a mere five cents can do when it's properly used?" he said. We oohed and aahed that this tiny adjustment could spell for Killy the difference between mere excellence and perfection. Or did it? A week or so later it occurred to me that maybe, just maybe, he had been kidding.

But, in fact, when it came to Killy, nothing was too outrageous to believe when it involved skiing. In his first four years of competition, from 1964 to 1967, he won all the legendary European races: the Arlberg-Kandahar, the

In the early Seventies, Vail was a regular stop on the hotdog skiing circuits. There were bump contests on Look Ma above Mid Vail (facing page) and aerial competitions that wowed the crowds and set the stage for modern freestyle skiing.

Hahnenkamm, and the Lauberhorn. Then he won the first World Cup competition in 1967, with a massive 225 points—the maximum possible under the rules that year. The next year he won the World Cup by a staggering 111 points over the runner-up. Following his Olympic blowout in 1968, he retired from ski racing at the age of twenty-four. In 1973 he came out of retirement for a single season of professional racing on Bob Beattie's pro circuit and won more races than anyone that year. Then having shown the world he was still King Killy, he retired again. I consider Jean-Claude the greatest athlete who skied at Vail during the glory years of the Sixties and early Seventies.

★ ★ ★ ★ ★

Possibly the achievement I relished most during our magic decade was the economic impact we made outside the resort. Because of Vail, all of Eagle County blossomed and grew—from East Vail to Gypsum, some forty miles along I-70. After showing signs of prosperity in the early years, the towns of Avon and Edwards simply exploded in the Eighties and Nineties, becoming affluent and progressive municipalities filled to the brim with shops, restaurants, condominiums, and houses.

Dramatic individual success stories also bloomed like wildflowers in that early time. For example, there was Gerald Gallegos, a native of Minturn, who started working during the summer of 1968, a high-school student turned stonemason with one old wheelbarrow and a rusty concrete maker. He was such a quick and careful worker that he was able to start his own business in 1970, specializing in small jobs, particularly fireplaces. He then founded Gallegos Masonry, Inc., and the number of employees grew to twenty, then one hundred. Today Gerald has four hundred people working for him and branch offices in Aspen, Telluride, and Sun Valley.

When Gastof Gramshammer was built in the early Sixties (right), there were only a few buildings in town. But with each passing year the pace of construction accelerated. By the Seventies (below), the center of Vail Village had began to look much as it does today.

★　★　★　★　★

Not only did Vail prosper in those years, but so did the entire Colorado ski industry. One reason for this was the cooperative marketing done by Colorado Ski Country USA, the association of Colorado resorts. The organization was the brainchild of my 10th Mountain Division buddy Steve Knowlton, who was its first executive director. The name itself was conceived by Bob Parker, who had used it in Vail's first marketing campaigns ("VAIL, COLORADO, SKI COUNTRY USA," the ads said.) At a meeting of the Southern Rockies Ski Areas Association in 1964, Steve Knowlton had asked me if the state association he was proposing could use the name. Neither Bob Parker nor I had any objection, and thus CSCUSA was born.

All sorts of firsts can be attributed to the association. It was the first ski-resort organization in the world dedicated to marketing and promotion, setting the stage for Ski Utah, Ski New England, and a host of others that followed. It was also the first to conduct independent research. A groundbreaking economic-impact study of the ski business and a study of the effects of

The Lodge at Vail was the premier hotel in the valley for many years. It was completed just in time for the opening season in 1962-63.

snowmaking on water supply were just two of CSCUSA's pioneering efforts.

★ ★ ★ ★ ★

We welcomed our one-millionth skier in the spring of 1968; our five-millionth in 1976. In December 1972 *Time* magazine published a cover story about the phenomenal worldwide boom in skiing, declaring: "The nation now has nearly 700 ski areas, double the number a decade ago. At least 6,000,000 Americans are skiers and the total is climbing 15 percent a year. Round the world more than 20 million people ski. For the world's resort owners, hotel operators, travel agents, equipment makers, clothing designers, real estate speculators and orthopedic surgeons, skiing this year will be a $10 billion enterprise."

Time chose Vail as the centerpiece for the story, calling it "an instant Alpine community that is the most successful winter resort built in the U.S. in the last decade." The magazine went on to explore both the pros and the cons of Vail's rapid growth:

As in any ski town there are problems of extreme expansion and contraction. The population swells from 700 in the summer to 10,000 in the winter. There is a shortage of moderate-income housing for Vail's ski instructors, waiters and salespeople, many of whom live in a trailer camp a dozen miles away. The permanent year-round residents who run the town are mostly conservative, family-oriented folk. They can afford to pay $35,000 or more for condominiums.

When Vail grew so big that it could no longer be run by Pete Seibert alone, he moved up from president to chairman and brought in Richard L. Peterson, a Harvard MBA. Last year the company grossed $6,700,000 from lifts, ski school, restaurants and land sales, and earned $812,000 after taxes. Expanding, it recently spent

THE FIRST TAKEOVER ATTEMPT

On September 23, 1968, a Denver investor and business consultant named James A. Krentler offered to buy 365,000 shares of Vail Associates, Inc. at $5 a share. He said he already held 71,390 shares of the 871,223 VA shares outstanding. That would make his total holding 436,390 shares—and give him a little over 50 percent of the stock. Among other things, Krentler was president of an investment company with the puzzling name of Unlimited Ltd. He was also on the executive committee of the board of directors of Great Western United Corp headed by William M. White Jr. Just a week before the takeover shot at us, Krentler and White had established a charitable fund called the Great Western United Foundation—

its sole aim, according to its prospectus, to "promote the general well-being of mankind."

To the VA board this takeover attempt was like a rabbit punch. I sent a letter to VA's stockholders, saying, "Vail's management recommends that you do not accept this offer. According to daily price quotations published in the Denver Post, Vail's common stock has traded on the over the counter market in Denver during the last four months at prices...that...don't represent either the present asset value of the company or its earning potential. If you sell your shares now, you will be denied the opportunity to participate in Vail's future..."

Krentler and his Great Western cohorts were never heard from again.

$4.6 million for 2,200 acres of Beaver Creek, seven miles from the main development: the area is scheduled to open in 1975. Seibert himself owns Vail stock worth more than $600,000. But, he insists: "Money is really not my thing. More important, I'm right where I have wanted to be since I was a kid."

* * * * *

Vail kept on prospering through the 1960s and into the 1970s. We were blessed with good snow in November most of the time, giving us early openings that made money—and also made friends of skiers everywhere. In 1968 we successfully headed off a takeover threat from a Denver investor whose company had the puzzling name Unlimited, Ltd.

Dick Peterson's arrival as president of Vail Associates freed me to pursue exciting new ventures, such as the purchase of neighboring Beaver Creek in 1971, and the acceptance of Vail and Beaver Creek as official venues for the proposed Colorado Winter Olympics in 1976. There had been considerable competition among resorts for the privilege of hosting Olympic events. Bob Parker and I had gone to Sapporo, Japan, in 1972 when the International Olympic Committee officially chose Colorado to host the next Winter Games. We envisioned glory and gold medals. Nine months later, however, the Olympics were voted down in a statewide referendum. Despite the blow, our reputation, our morale, and our profits continued to soar. Then came another blow on a bright March day in 1976, and we had to face the fact that we were not invulnerable to terrible events. Indeed, for all practical purposes, I came to the end of my dream because of what happened that day. **V**▫

"SARGE" BROWN AND THE PILOT OF RENOWN

Bill "Sarge" Brown, Vail's mountain manager for close to thirty years, played a key role in the resort's success. A 10th Mountain Division veteran, he was "about as tough a young man as you could find in the whole outfit," says Bob Parker. He rose in the ranks quickly, becoming the youngest first sergeant in the army. He fought in the Italian campaign, earned a Silver Star, and was seriously wounded just days before the end of the war. During the Korean War he went back into the army, got another Silver Star, and decided to make the army his career.

In the mid Sixties he volunteered for Vietnam but was turned down.

Left to right: Pete Seibert, Bob Parker, Bill Brown

Angry, he quit the army and called Bob Parker and me, looking for a job. We put him on as head of a trail crew. Within months he was running the entire slope-maintenance department, and before long he was mountain manager and then director of mountain operations.

He raised the job to a higher level, found ingenious ways to improve slope-grooming procedures and equipment, ran world-class international races, and expected a lot from his crews. A tough taskmaster, he rarely gave compliments—and certainly never to women. Except once.

One spring I suggested to Brown that he consider hiring a crop duster to fertilize and seed the cleared trails instead of doing it the usual way by hand. Bill said he'd check it out and next thing I knew he had an estimate on his desk indicating that a crop duster would be both cheaper and faster.

Several days later a low wing crop duster stood beside U.S. Highway 6 with a fuel truck and bags of fertilizer ready for use on the mountain.

The pilot, a woman in her fifties, was geared up and ready to fly. After each hair-raising descent down the winding trails, she would return, land on the highway, top off the gas tank, pick up grass seed and fertilizer and head back up the mountain. To spectators it looked like part of an aerial circus. What a show!

When the job was done (in a tenth of the usual time), I asked Bill for his opinion of both the results and the pilot. "Pretty damned good," said Brown. "And that lady pilot is one hell of a tough broad!"

The lady never knew she'd received Bill Brown's ultimate compliment.

Pete Seibert in Game Creek Bowl, early Seventies.

CHAPTER ELEVEN

TRAGEDY ON THE MOUNTAIN

My office was on the second floor of the Lionshead administration building, just below the Gondola II terminal. On this day, March 26, 1976, I glanced idly out my windows at the unusually long morning liftlines that were forming for the gondola. I wasn't surprised or concerned, because it was a beautiful sunny morning, a perfect skiing day. It was also spring vacation for schools throughout the country, and hundreds of families were at Vail.

Then I noticed that the gondola wasn't running. The brightly colored cabins dangled like jellybeans above the dazzling snowy slopes. It wasn't unusual, however, for the cars to stop from time to time, for a variety of reasons. It crossed my mind that this would be a bad day for the gondola to need repairs, but I didn't dwell on it and went back to work.

Maybe two minutes later the phone rang. I glanced to see if the gondola was moving yet. It wasn't. I picked up the phone; the call was from ski patrol headquarters. A voice said calmly, "An accident on the gondola. Tower Five. Cars have fallen. We don't know about casualties yet."

"Everybody's on it?" I asked.

"Everybody on the mountain."

"Keep me posted. I'm staying here."

A reflex kicked in that I had developed during my years in the 10th Mountain Division: Don't panic in the face of a crisis; stay where you are; don't move until you know what has happened. As a former ski patrolman, I would have liked to have grabbed a snowmobile and gone right to the site of the accident. But the best men were already up there. My job was here.

My first call was to the Vail hospital to find out if they knew of the accident. They were already in the process of informing the Flight for Life operation in Denver that helicopters might be needed to bring badly hurt victims to the better-equipped hospitals there. From then on, as the dark hours of this initially brilliant day inched past, I stayed at my desk, near the phone.

On that day, March 26, 1976, passengers were stranded in cars the full length of the gondola line, but two cars hung precariously more than 100 feet above the ground. The lattice-style towers were typical of the European-made gondolas of the time.

Slowly the terrible truth became clear. Two of our gondola cars, each carrying a capacity load of six skiers, had gotten snagged on frayed cable. After being thrown about briefly, they fell 125 feet to the ground at the base of a tower. Three people were dead: two teenage girls and a woman. The other nine passengers were injured, some severely.

After the two cars fell, the two cars behind them collided at the tower, came to a jarring halt, and now dangled precariously. At intervals all the way up and down the 9,274-foot-long gondola line other cars hung from the cable, some as high as 170 feet in the air. In all, 176 people were stranded.

A woman—unknown to this day—saw the cars fall and made the first call to the patrol from an emergency phone on the Born Free run. She was hysterical and spoke with an accent; the dispatcher made her repeat the message. Then his call went out immediately. I followed with calls directing specific people to specific positions.

Snowcat drivers got the word, as did every ski instructor, lift operator, policeman, fireman, and all medical center personnel. Ambulance drivers started their engines and snowplow drivers prepared to clear back roads where emergency equipment might have to travel.

A skier told a patroller what the accident looked like from the ground (as quoted in a subsequent *Sports Illustrated* story): "One gondola car banged hard against the tower, veered away, then slammed against it again. I saw sparks and an odd white powder, like snow. I watched as the car fell. Like an apple from a tree. No, like a feather. It separated from the cable and fell slowly. Then a second car approached and slammed into the tower. There were people inside. They beat their fists against the glass. Then they fell, too."

Left: Assistant patrol director John Murphy watches as patroller Chupa Nelson, standing on the disabled cars, attaches first a rope, then a chain, to secure the cars to the overhead cable. Above: Two cars fell from the cable that fateful day, resulting in four deaths.

CHAPTER TWELVE

BEAVER CREEK

In the aftermath of the gondola accident, the inevitable happened: By the summer of 1976 we were being sued for more than $50 million in damages—way beyond the net worth of the whole company. Repair of the Lionshead gondola and replacement of the Vail Village gondola cost over $3 million. And we were on the brink of starting to develop our new sister resort, Beaver Creek. There was also concern that we might face a hostile takeover since we had been so successful in the past fifteen years. It was a daunting situation.

I was still chairman of the board, but maintaining control was not easy. I agreed with the consensus of the board members that we should search for a buyer at the right price. But the board was more afraid of the immense liability we might incur as a result of the accident than of any other costs.

In September 1976, less than six months after the gondola cars fell, the Vail Associates board fell, too. We sold the company to board member Harry Bass, a Texas millionaire. His money came mostly from his family's ownership of Goliad Oil and Gas. He and his brother Dick had owned Vail stock from the moment we issued it in 1966. Dick offered to sell Harry his place on the board, and Harry later explained to the press, "I had already started buying Vail shares, so I had a pretty good block. I think I topped out at around eight or nine percent, something like that. So I took Dick's seat on the board. Vail didn't have an ownership leader."

Harry wound up with 52 percent of the shares and offered to buy Vail Associates. And we couldn't deny that we needed capital.

I personally didn't favor Harry Bass. And, in fact, Twentieth Century Fox was very interested in buying Vail. But the studio hadn't yet released its blockbuster movie *ET* and lacked the cash to match Bass's bid. So Vail went to the big guy from Texas.

Harry and I had a difficult relationship. A humungous

In the late Seventies, before Beaver Creek opened, Vail Associates ran informal snowcat tours of the new mountain. For the fortunate few who took advantage of the opportunity, every tour (such as this one in March 1979) was a voyage of discovery, and every run a feast of untracked powder.

personality clash, I guess you'd call it. A couple of days after he took over, he asked me to lunch at an outdoor restaurant in Lionshead. There was an odd, stiff air about our meeting, and I decided to tell him a joke that would either loosen him up or make him mad as hell.

"Harry," I said. "There was this old New England farmer who was visiting a big old rancher in west Texas. The farmer saw a strange-looking bird scurrying along a fence line, and he said to the Texan, 'What's that?'

"'That's the bird of paradise,' said the rancher.

"The New Englander stared at the bird for a moment, then burst out, 'Gawddamn! He sure is a hel-luva long way from home.'"

Harry not only didn't laugh, but he sort of growled, "You oughta have learned by now, Pete. New England humor doesn't travel well."

It turned out Harry had asked me to lunch to fire me, so he then asked me, "You know what git-along means, Pete?"

I shrugged and said nothing.

"Git-along means you got to get along, Pete. You got to get a long, long way from here. Goodbye."

As he got up from the table, I wished him well and said that I hoped he'd take good care of Vail.

I went back to my office and picked up a few personal items: pictures of my kids, a golf trophy, a ski trophy, and an album of pictures illustrating my history at Vail. Then I went home to see what else might happen. Early the next morning a Vail Associates truck rolled into my driveway full of everything I had left in my office, including the desk, rolling chair, filing cabinets, and wastebasket.

A couple of former employees unloaded it all into my garage. One had tears in his eyes; I did, too. When I started Vail, I didn't necessarily plan on making a lifetime commitment. But when I had to leave, I suddenly discovered that I'd made a much deeper commitment than I had realized. It really hurt to go.

For the first few years after Beaver Creek opened, the village at the base was a construction zone. So Spruce Saddle, the beautifully designed restaurant at mid mountain, became the focal point for guests at the resort. Even novice skiers used Spruce Saddle as their base for the day, because the trails above it were so easy to handle.

* * * * *

It hurt all the more a year or so later when the final legal results of the gondola disaster were announced: The anticipated massive deluge of damage payments had not come to pass. The total payout was only a fraction of the $50 million we had been sued for, slightly more than $12 million in all. And most of the costs were covered by insurance. Now it really galled me to realize that we had let the place go to Harry Bass for a song because of our misjudgment on what the damage suits would cost.

However, Harry and the executives he hired had stumbled into some misjudgments of their own. The most serious had to do with Beaver Creek, a place that had come to be very close to my heart. Indeed, the blueprints for Beaver Creek were the most precious items I left behind as a legacy for Harry Bass.

Earl Eaton and I had actually explored the mountain as far back as 1957, and we had agreed that it might even be a better ski mountain than Vail. At the time, we put it on a back burner while we concentrated on the big one, but we never forgot it. This vast, untouched mountain was just eight miles from Vail, a magnificent 2,200-acre mix of rolling woodsy slopes, gentle mountain meadows, and screamingly steep drops.

It remained a sleeping kingdom until 1971. Then it was time

BEAVER CREEK'S TRAILS

Despite the chaos and bad management that plagued Beaver Creek in its early years, the village has risen out of the dust to be one of the most luxurious resorts in the world, with particularly elegant and imaginative architecture. The mountain has become one of skiing's best, including a marvelous network of beginner summit runs, giving novices the kind of views usually attainable only by stronger skiers. Most of Beaver Creek's other runs are groomed but fairly steep—ego trips for intermediates. The knee-wrenching moguls on Grouse Mountain are an exception. Opened in 1990, Grouse matches the best black trails of Vail.

There are also the mind-blowing, 2,100-foot drop-offs called the Birds of Prey. In his book *Mountain Vision: The Making of Beaver Creek*, Seth Marx lavished them with praise:

Named after three impressive flying raptors that live in the region, the Birds of Prey trails offer unimaginable challenges and great rewards. The double diamond trails have claimed their fair share of broken limbs and disheartened skiers' souls over the years, but they have also treated many powder hounds to endless fresh tracks. Goshawk, Peregrine and Golden Eagle drop over 2,100 feet from top to bottom.

During the 1999 FIS World Championships, the Birds of Prey were the centerpiece of the downhill, which started at the moderate slopes of the summit, then suddenly fell away at the Birds and hit drop-offs as steep as the side of a skyscraper. Nothing made me prouder than to watch those great racers tackling the mountain I had discovered almost forty-five years ago.

In fact, the Birds of Prey course was the result of an exhaustive study I had done in the mid 1990s to find a challenging new downhill. I looked first at Vail Mountain, then at Marvin's Chutes, east of China Bowl outside the Vail Mountain boundary, then at Beaver Creek. My realization of the world-class Beaver Creek terrain, coupled with the expertise of Bernhard Russi, an Olympic medalist and pre-eminent race course designer, resulted in a great challenge for today's downhill racers.

It is almost hard to believe that I had ranked this magnificent mountain behind Vail in the late 1950s. But I still believe that Vail Mountain was the best first choice. With its vast, dramatic Back Bowls and the groomed slopes of the front side, no hill in the world is more fun to ski.

to awaken it and transform it into one of the most luxurious resorts in the world. As CEO of Vail, I engineered the purchase of Beaver Creek by Vail Associates. The price was $4.4 million, a deal won only after years of jawing and gnawing and chewing tobacco with the owner of the land we needed, a stubborn old rancher named Willis Nottingham.

Once Nottingham finalized the sale in '71, we were ready to develop the area. We had our permit requests ready to go, and the Forest Service was inclined to grant them. We also had the money. The only thing wrong was our timing, which coincided with the infamous collapse of the Colorado Winter Olympics planned for 1976.

No one told the story more succinctly than Paul Hauk of the Forest Service, our old friend and sometime nemesis from the years when we started Vail. He produced an eleven-page, single-spaced report of all that went on, declaring in the first paragraph:

This chronology is primarily a history of confrontations dating back to late 1967 and Denver's successful bid for the 1976 Winter Olympics. That designation led to the political and environmental in-fighting regarding the sites for the various events, especially Alpine and cross-country skiing. The Alpine conflict began in earnest in 1970 and ended in February 1972, when Beaver Creek was finally designated after the choices bounced between Mt. Sniktau [near Loveland ski area] and Copper Mountain. Nine months later, on November 7, 1972, nearly 900,000 voters by a 3 to 2 margin approved the state Referendum Initiative and killed the '76 Winter Games for Denver and Colorado—something that had never happened anywhere since the modern Games were revived in 1896.

was finally issued by the Forest Service on March 22, 1976."

It was a long, and expensive, football game. We had spent about $6 million on the project. The estimated interest on the money we had borrowed from a Denver bank was $425,000 a year. After I left the company, new owner Harry Bass had no choice but to keep on spending to keep that football in the air for everyone to kick. We had hoped we could get to work and open for the 1977–'78 season. But there was no chance. The state of Colorado asked the Forest Service to hold off on issuing the permit, claiming it violated the service's own guidelines and that it would cause the "urbanization" of the upper Eagle Valley.

The true confrontation at this point was between the Forest Service and the state. Vail Associates tried to be open-minded and listen to the changes demanded by environmentalists and other ostensibly hostile forces. As Bob Parker said to Seth H. Marx, author of *Mountain Vision, The Making of Beaver Creek*, "We were broad-minded enough to recognize the right of the public to participate, the right of environmental groups to be involved, and we were willing to sit down and work things out. There are very few owners who have ever been willing to take that position and sort of live that philosophy. I think that is one of the unique things about Vail Associates."

Ultimately, the Forest Service issued the permits, and on July 28, 1977, the ceremonial groundbreaking took place on the site of Beaver Creek Village. Among those present were Harry Bass; President Gerald Ford; Jack Marshall, a California developer whom Harry had hired as president of Vail Associates; and White River Forest Supervisor Tom Evans, who had ruled for Vail time and again in those embattled years. Evans was an

Well, that was it in a nutshell: confrontation, contest, and infighting, followed by—what else?—a killing. I had greatly looked forward to creating a true Olympic village at Beaver Creek, doing it right from scratch. And I had looked forward to designing trails—Olympic trails—over that vast terrain. But we were left empty-handed: no Olympic races at Beaver Creek and no Forest Service permission to build lifts and trails and buildings, either.

Hauk wrote: "Vail Associates was, as one magazine put it, 'Up the creek without a permit.' Beaver Creek literally became a political football for the next three years, until the special-use permit

enthusiastic fan of our environmental attitudes, and he said that day: "Vail Associates has responsibly participated for two years in the most thorough and sensitive analysis involving winter resort planning that we have ever seen in Colorado."

Also present was Colorado Governor Dick Lamm, a tenacious, charismatic fellow who had led the environmental protesters in killing the Olympic Games and who had fought against Beaver Creek from its inception. But Lamm had been forced to knuckle under to federal regulation in the Beaver Creek case, and he now prided himself as being highly instrumental in persuading Vail Associates to come up with an inspired model of environmental development for Beaver Creek. At the ceremony, he raved, "Like Tiffany is to jewelry, like Gucci is to luggage, like Cadillac is to automobiles, that's what Beaver Creek is going to be to ski areas in this country." To us these remarks seemed hypocritical, considering all the years Lamm had spent fighting Beaver Creek.

* * * * *

Despite the triumphant ceremonies ushering in the Tiffany/Gucci/Cadillac era of ski resorts, trouble lay ahead. Beaver Creek opened in 1980 without a single shop, restaurant, or bed to rent. The main structure for skiers was a tennis bubble. Harry Bass had instituted an exhausting dash to the opening, and the place simply wasn't ready.

Thus Beaver Creek didn't generate anywhere near the kind of money necessary to finish it. Vail Associates boasted that some $500 million would be spent in the '80s to bring Beaver Creek to its dazzling finish. That first season attracted only 111,000 skiers and produced paltry real estate sales—profits from which were to be the ultimate source of the money needed to complete the resort.

As the Harry Bass years passed, he seemed to be running Vail Associates into the ground a little deeper every day. As Seth H. Marx wrote in his book, *Mountain Vision*, "The potential for profits at the new resort was grim for the short term, and Harry Bass and the rest of the board of directors began to worry in 1981 about how long the company could afford to wait. They had underestimated how much money and time it would take to get the resort to begin paying for itself, and the

Bass plan for Beaver Creek needed immediate adjustments."

The first adjustment Harry made was to appoint himself chief of real estate sales until May 1982, when he hired Harry Frampton, who had experience with real estate in Hilton Head, South Carolina, and Virginia. Frampton would say later (as quoted in *Mountain Vision*), "The reason they hired me was that they needed somebody to turn around Beaver Creek real estate or VA was going to go under."

It was that bad. Everything had stalled, and the major buildings in the village, such as Village Hall and the Poste Montane Lodge (which became known as the "Postpone Montane"), had a variety of troubles. After Frampton inspected the sites, he reported: "At the Village Hall project, the contractor had walked off the job. The Post Montane… had stopped because of cost overruns, the sheriff's office had tacked lien waivers all over the building…. Creekside Condominiums had run out of money…. The Charter was about a third complete and had been stopped by the lending bank."

For the next couple of years, not a lot of real estate moved. Much of it was overpriced, and the economy of the '80s was not conducive to big real estate projects. Over time, however, Harry Frampton managed to radically improve the company's real estate operations, and, in fact, all aspects of its operating procedures.

Then in 1984 a new force came to bear: The members of the board of the Goliad trust, which had been set up for the nine Bass children (Harry's children and their cousins), were worried. The directors decided that the Bass kids' main financial resources should not be utterly dependent on an investment in something as risky as Beaver Creek. The Goliad directors decided to pull their money out of Vail Associates.

Harry argued that the long-term investment potential of Vail and Beaver Creek was "as good as gold," but the trustees didn't agree. They gave him the boot as chairman of Vail Associates and went looking for someone with about $130 million to buy Vail and its debts as well as its troubled sister resort.

Harry (now deceased) never set foot in Vail again. **V**.

Beaver Creek's international coming-out party occurred in 1989 during the World Alpine Ski Championships.
Hundreds of journalists from around the world came to watch the races and enjoy Beaver Creek's unique amenities.

HEART OF THE ROCKIES

The Clock Tower is to Vail what the lower Manhattan skyline is to New York: a symbol of the town. But getting it built in the mid Sixties wasn't a sure thing, because some members of the architectural review board considered it too tall.

After my abrupt departure from Vail in 1976, I signed on as manager of the Country Club of the Rockies in Colorado Springs, running the restaurants and operating the golf course, tennis courts, and pools. I had recently been divorced, and not only did I miss Vail but I missed my family. But at least I was involved in sports that I liked, and being next to the Broadmoor Hotel, where many of my friends were a part of the management team, wasn't all that bad.

Then one day in the summer of 1978, Rod Slifer phoned from his real estate office in Vail: Jack Nicklaus had expressed interest in acquiring a ski area. Did I know of any areas for sale? And would I like to run it? My answers were yes and yes!

Two areas on the market at that time were in complete contrast: Northstar, near Lake Tahoe in California, was small, well designed, nicely maintained—and entirely on private land, so there would be no Forest Service bureaucracy to deal with.

Snowbasin, near Ogden, Utah, was much larger, with 2,900 vertical feet, wonderful slopes, and sprawling acres of private land to expand into. It was a true Alpine resort. But it was old—it had been a state playground and park since 1936—and had been poorly cared for over the years. As it happened, Northstar got tied up in legal matters that kept it off the market, so we went with Snowbasin.

By this time, however, Jack Nicklaus had seen the high-risk, low-profit financial status of many ski areas and was no longer interested in having one of his own. Slifer and I went ahead anyway, bringing in thirty-five investors to provide the $2.6 million we would need to buy and improve the ski area and option adjacent properties.

We contracted to purchase about 8,500 acres of private land contiguous to Snowbasin's Forest Service permit boundary, where we planned to develop a year-round mountain resort. The base site was perfect for a small Alpine village—there were wonderful intermediate slopes above— and the vast rolling acreage below the village site was ideal for golf and summer amenities. We called the proposed plan Trappers Loop, a name given to the region in its early days.

It was too ambitious a scheme to pull off with our limited resources, however. The financial burden of acquiring the 8,500 acres, coupled with the cost of running the ski area, finally put us under. The Ogden skier market was too small, and we weren't able to attract Salt Lake City skiers, despite the great slopes for all levels of skiers. And raising lift ticket prices would have cost us the local crowd.

We should have brought in a strong financial partner from the start. But we hadn't, and by the summer of 1984, with no white knight on the horizon, we went looking for a buyer. It was clear that the only way our original investors could get so

UTAH NIGHTS IN THE SHOOTING STAR SALOON

Maybe the best-known location for good times in northern Utah is the Shooting Star Saloon in Huntsville, a small farming community in the valley below Snowbasin. Though nondrinkers are the norm here, the Shooting Star is a monument the community is more or less proud of—it's the oldest bar in Utah, quite an accomplishment considering the state's complicated liquor laws.

It's a joint with true Western character: a long wooden bar; bacon rinds, pickled pigs' feet, and hard-boiled eggs in jars; a pool table in the back of the room; and a juke box with the Sons of the Pioneers singing "Cool Water." But what gives the Shooting Star its true authenticity is the line-up of stuffed animal heads hanging from one wall: moose, foxes, coyotes, wolves, elk, cougar, and—the centerpiece—the head of a St. Bernard with a cigarette dangling from its mouth.

Next to the Shooting Star is a feed store; the back wall is contiguous to the bar wall lined with heads. My friends and I would discuss our plans to buy the feed store, put in a restaurant called the Falling Star Saloon, and mount hindquarters to match the heads hanging in the Shooting Star. We would call this the Rump Room.

Around 10 P.M. on really busy nights, the Rattlesnake Olympics would begin, when one of the braver—or drunker—patrons would open the acquarium behind the bar. Coiled inside were two or three rattlesnakes. Someone would reach in and gingerly pull out the snakes, one by one, and place them on the end of the bar. The whole place would then bet on which snake could crawl the full fifteen-foot length of the bar. Sometimes none could, sometimes all did, sometimes one fell off the bar and disappeared. And sometimes a drinker would send everyone scrambling when he yelled, "Hey! Weren't there three snakes?"

much as a dime of their money back was for us to sell the area. But who would buy it? And for how much?

I considered possible buyers, and I could only come up with one man who might be interested, Earl Holding, owner of Sinclair Oil, the Little America Hotel chain, and Sun Valley. I didn't even know what he looked like at this point. I was close to going broke, with only eight hundred dollars in the bank, and I didn't expect another paycheck from Snowbasin ever again. I decided that I had to meet Holding in a casual way— and as an equal. In no way could I even remotely resemble a dead-broke entrepreneur begging him to buy Snowbasin. So I withdrew six hundred dollars of my meager funds to cover the entry fee to a golf tournament that was to be held at Sun Valley in a month. I figured that I'd meet Holding there, befriend

George Gillett, Vail's energetic owner during the second half of the Eighties, invested $65 million in the resort, opened the huge China Bowl, and brought international attention by staging the 1989 World Alpine Ski Championships.

developing Arrowhead at Vail, a new resort next to Beaver Creek. Wright asked me to design the trails and lifts, keeping in mind that someday they would be a logical extension of the Beaver Creek/Bachelor Gulch expansion already on the drawing boards at Vail Associates. Arrowhead offered the last really skiable terrain in the western extremes of the Vail Valley.

We put up a great-looking Doppelmayr quad lift as the centerpiece and installed snowmaking as the Western/Alpine base village took shape. All of it blended beautifully with Vail's Alpine style and Beaver Creek's European-flavored resort village.

Arrowhead at Vail opened in 1985. As it turned out, the ski area may have been a bit ahead of its time. Progress in real estate was slow in spite of a challenging new Jack Nicklaus golf course that had just opened. But in 1992 Vail Associates did what we had hoped for: they bought Arrowhead and, in doing so, put the final piece in place in the ultimate development of the Vail Valley.

And it turned out that I, too, was still considered an integral piece of the Vail operation. Fittingly enough, given the emphasis I had always placed on racing at Vail, my return to Vail associates happened on the most triumphant day of racing that Vail had ever had: February 12, 1989, the final day of the FIS World Alpine Ski Championships. The prize ceremonies were coming to an end, and I was standing at the rear of the stage, not far from George Gillett, who was fairly beaming with happiness. These championships—the first held in the U.S. since that long-ago competition in Aspen in 1950—had gone beautifully, and Vail now commanded new respect from the Europeans who ruled international ski racing.

George turned to me. "What a day!" he cried. He then looked me in the eye, grabbed my shoulders in a bear hug, and shouted, "Pete! When are you coming back?"

"Coming back?"

"Back to work for Vail Associates. We need you, fella."

I'd been waiting quite a while for something like this to happen. I laughed and said, "Sounds great. Let me think about it. I'll get back to you soon, George."

I paused for a full five seconds while George frowned slightly, then said, "Okay, it's a deal. Where's my office?"

him, and convince him to at least visit Snowbasin to see if he might want to buy it.

It worked. Within a couple of weeks Earl Holding and his family were climbing all over Snowbasin, kicking lift towers, studying ski runs, checking the condition of area snowcats and snowmobiles. He asked a million questions. No wonder he was such a success; he didn't leave a stone unturned. Rod Slifer came over from Vail to negotiate the deal, but there was nothing, really, to negotiate. We took the terms that Earl offered.

Subsequently Snowbasin was selected to host the downhill and super G races for the Salt Lake City 2002 Winter Olympics, and for the second time I lost a chance to be involved in designing an Olympic venue and hosting a Winter Games.

Sometimes I wish to hell I could have survived at Snowbasin to see this crowning triumph. The downhill course was designed by Swiss Olympic gold medalist Bernard Russi, one of the best downhill racers in the world twenty years ago and today considered one of the best designers of downhill courses. At Snowbasin, Russi carved the run around pre-existing obstacles—glacial rocks, mammoth tree trunks—and he let it fall over heart-stopping 70 percent grades, with a vertical drop of 2,900 feet.

Oh, well, let the Games begin!

* * * * *

When I left Utah in 1984, I moved back to share in the action going on in the Vail area. My old friend Jen Wright, a real estate man who had worked for Vail Associates in the past, was

Beaver Creek now. The seemingly endless construction, false starts, and financial struggles of the Seventies and Eighties have given way to a Swiss-style village featuring high-end luxury accommodation and great skiing on the mountain.

George Gillett was a likeable guy. He was also an ambitious and an energetic guy. In 1989 Rod Slifer, when asked by *Sports Illustrated* to compare the various Vail Associates' regimes, had said "I think Peter and George Gillett have similarities. The mountain and skiing interest them, and the quality of skiing comes first. Harry Bass ran it like a business. He didn't put money back in the mountain, he drained it off. Pete and George believe in the European idea of business: Think of the future, think of your kids. This isn't a place to grab instant profits, it's a long-term investment. I think George Gillett might be the best owner Vail ever had. He has lots of money, he has lots of contact with the town, he makes people here feel good."

THE APOLLO FAMILY

The owners of Vail like to spin off intracompany corporations under a variety of similar names. For example, Apollo Advisors, Apollo Ski Partners, Inc., Apollo Capital Management, and Apollo Fund are all company branches. Sheri Cole, a reporter for the *Vail Trail,* explained it this way:

Vail Resorts, Inc., a Delaware corporation, owns Vail Associates and Vail Resorts Development Company. (VA runs the ski mountain operations and VRDC develops and manages the company's real estate holdings.) VR is a publicly traded company with two types of out-

standing stock—common stock and Class A common stock.... Apollo Ski Partners was organized for the purpose of holding VR stock. The general partner of Apollo Ski Partners is Apollo Fund, a Delaware limited partnership and a private securities investment fund. The managing general partner of Apollo Fund is Apollo Advisers, a Delaware limited partnership, the general partner of which is Apollo Capital Management, Inc., another Delaware corporation.

Finally, a French company called Artemis is a major investor in Apollo projects. In Greek mythology, Artemis is Apollo's twin sister.

But three years after the World Championships, no one in town was feeling very good about George. His vast TV kingdom had serious problems; he had borrowed big throughout the 1980s, first to accumulate the stations, then to keep them afloat in ever-rising red ink. He got his financial backing from junk-bond czar Michael Milken and from Drexel Burnham Lambert, Inc., the well-known (and now-defunct) Wall Street firm that underwrote those bonds.

George's company, Gillett Holdings, Inc., which officially owned Vail, issued millions of dollars in junk bonds underwritten by Drexel Burnham. Some of those bonds were burdened with interest rates as high as 17.5 percent. When TV advertising revenue continued to sink, George couldn't even pay the interest in some cases. Talk of bankruptcy began as early as November 1989. He fought it off at first, then surrendered and declared Chapter 11 bankruptcy in June 1991 and Chapter 7 personal bankruptcy a year later. Ultimately, he had defaulted on debts of more than $1 billion.

Ever the optimist, George insisted that Vail's operations would not be affected, saying, "The figures from this past season (1991–92) show that, once again, Vail and Beaver Creek were the nation's favorite ski resorts in terms of attendance. We fully intend to continue that momentum and to live up to our commitment to excellence." And when someone asked him about the greatest piece of advice he had received during the years of financial upheaval, he chuckled and said, "Just because someone is willing to lend you money doesn't mean you should borrow it."

With great reluctance, George Gillett sold Vail in 1992 for $130 million to pay a portion of his debts.

* * * * *

The new owner was Apollo Advisors, an investment firm founded in August 1990 by Leon D. Black and several partners. Before Apollo, Black had been a managing director at Drexel Burnham Lambert, where he had headed mergers and acquisitions and had been the co-head of corporate finance. Apollo recapitalized the bankrupt Gillett Holdings by putting in equity. The company then sold the TV stations, the meat packing operations, and the excess land holdings, leaving the firm with just Vail Associates.

Personally, I was uneasy about the new ownership, and I was very sorry to see George go. After all, he had brought me back to Vail Associates after all those years in the wilderness. Also I wasn't

sure that a powerful private equity firm was the right entity to run something as unpredictable and, at times, as unmanageable as a ski resort. Big-time corporate techniques wouldn't necessarily apply, and bottom-line thinking couldn't always be used as the final judgment of success. I was afraid the MBA mentality might not appreciate the need to expand and improve our mountains to make the skiing ever more exciting. And I didn't know if the importance of Alpine ski racing would be understood.

One thing was certain: Both Vail and Beaver Creek were in great shape when Apollo entered the picture because George had spent $65 million to enhance the mountains. Improvements included the opening of China Bowl, new quad lifts, and the addition of the magnificent expert trails on

Overnight visitors to Beaver Creek in the Eighties usually took the shuttle bus to Vail every night, because Beaver Creek had so little going on after dark. Now Beaver Creek even has its own performing arts theater.

Beaver Creek's Grouse Mountain. Also, there had been a steady increase in visits over the past five years, from 1,285,195 skiers in 1987 to 1,540,018 in 1992.

It took a while for the corporate managers and the mountain managers to meld. We were alien to each other at first. All sorts of efforts were made to make us comfortable together: get-acquainted cocktail parties, meetings with town officials, cookouts, picnics. It was all a little artificial, but eventually we became more trusting of each other.

I remember meeting Leon Black for the first time at an evening barbecue at Mid Vail. I was impressed with his questions and with his general air of confidence about operating Vail. His wife and children were with him. They were all skiers. I said to Leon, "It looks to me as if you and your family are already hooked on Vail. It's not just another corporation, it's a home, Leon."

He laughed. "Yeah, I know. We're going to love this place."

* * * * *

My fears that the new proprietors might become impatient and cancel costly plans to develop major projects such as Bachelor Gulch, Blue Sky Basin, or the purchase of Arrowhead proved to be absolutely groundless. Apollo executives charged ahead with something like the same verve George Gillett—or I—would have shown.

Marc Rowan, a founding principal of Apollo Advisors, laid down the company line: "We're going to complete Beaver Creek as planned, and we're going to acquire Arrowhead, which would have happened long ago except that George Gillett and Issam Fares, owner of the area, never could agree on anything. We're committed to the village-to-village skiing model and to the completion of Blue Sky Basin. We're diversifying the company by building retail business with the Gart family [who developed the Gart Brothers chain of sporting goods stores] and by acquiring the Lodge at Vail and The Pines at Beaver Creek."

And to my great joy, when the time came to bid for the 1999 FIS World Championships, Apollo's new owners agreed with us old owners that we had to go all out to get them. And we did.

All of this was close enough to my old dream to give me a

great sense of satisfaction and excitement. I had hoped that Vail Mountain would always be full of new surprises and new ideas. And damned if Apollo didn't come through.

Then in the summer of 1996 Leon Black startled everyone with a bombshell business deal: a $310-million merger between Vail Resorts and Ralston Resorts, a ski-area subsidiary of the massive manufacturer of brands like Chex and Purina. This gave Vail Resorts control of Breckenridge and Keystone, our long-time rivals thirty miles closer to Denver who had often siphoned off our customers.

At about the same time, Black decided to issue an initial public offering (IPO) of Vail Resorts, Inc. stock. Business writer Christopher Byron produced a hair-raising report on Black's move in the September 1996 issue of *Snow Country* magazine:

> In taking Vail Resorts public, Black's cashing in on the so-called 'IPO fever' that has been sweeping Wall Street for more than a year. [But] the fact is, if one were to hunt the canyons of Wall Street for the worst conceivable investment, the ski industry would seem to fit the bill. It's a seasonal business subject to the whims of weather. It labors under high capital costs and huge liability exposure. Its longtime customers are aging and its market is flat. And every effort to attract business by expanding terrain or building new resorts brings screams of outrage from angry environmentalists.

It was a blood-curdling description of the ski business. Yet Black and Apollo remained positive about their plans for the future.

* * * * *

I like to divide the life of Vail into three periods. During the first ten years, 1962 to 1972, it was a rustic settlement, and we were a high-spirited family of romantic pioneers who filled the Eagle Valley with optimism and an almost childlike innocence and generosity. (Cynics may find that description nauseating, but I refuse to back down from it.) We also made a lot of money and created a world-class ski resort. These were the "beyond belief years."

During the second period, 1973 to 1984, waves of new people came to town to build on the foundation laid by us pioneers. Some of them turned out to be opportunists, who invested, made money, and left. The amount of building was phenomenal, and, even

Facing page: When Vail bought Breckenridge in 1996, the one-time mining town was already experiencing a renaissance. Since then the resort's popularity has exploded. Right: Adam Aron, Vail Resorts chairman and CEO, who joined the company in 1996.

Keystone opened in 1972 as a modest-sized mountain with easy runs. Today Keystone encompasses three mountains, with ski terrain for every ability level and two separate base areas, including the new River Run complex at right.

though it generated profit as well as some questionable architecture, some of the early settlers chose to move away to escape the roar of bulldozers and the steadily spreading carpet of condominiums. Still, the mountain offered magnificent skiing, while remaining an utterly family-oriented resort, and Vail received accolades from ski writers around the world. These were the "sweet and sour years."

The third period, 1985 to the present, saw some marvelous development and on-mountain expansion: China Bowl and Blue Sky Basin, among others. Real estate boomed, and our population of millionaires per square foot was probably exceeded only by St. Moritz or Aspen. But there was also a lively sense of

At Breckenridge you get what you see: the resort's extensive trail system stretches along a section of the Ten Mile Range in full view of the town.

vitality about the place, a deeply rooted optimism. Vail was a resort for the millennium: irrefutably better groomed, better designed, and better run than any ski area on earth. These are the "future-is-now years."

Some time ago I became hooked on the idea of writing a book about my life and times, with the emphasis on the discovery of Vail Mountain and the ultimate dream that it enabled. Neither Earl Eaton nor I were much good at documenting long-range ideas. I guess the only tangible evidence of our vision other than the town and the mountains themselves was the scale model of the mountain we had built to show prospective investors. The model, about three feet by five feet, displayed in topographic detail the terrain included in the Forest Service permit. It was, unfortunately, lost in the ensuing years.

Somehow this magic, miniature Vail Mountain had managed to contain all of our passionate plans and heartfelt hopes for the future as it looked to us forty-three years ago.

But that future is now, and I am a happy man. Vail is in good hands. My family—including three sons, two daughters-in-law, and five grandchildren—is well, and most everyone is marvelously skilled at my beloved sport of ski racing. The grandchildren—two boys and three girls—have racked up many medals in junior alpine competitions over the years, and they are just getting started. The Seiberts have lived in this Colorado Camelot for most of their lives and most of them wouldn't trade it, no matter what its imperfections may be.

How do you bring such a story to a close? You don't. You just let it go on and on. Hell, I'm only seventy-five! **V**

1968

2000

1976

1993

1970

1995

1992

1981

1996

1998

1982

1973

1989

1990

1973

1985

1993

1992

THE PRESS BOX
How Others Saw Us

Over the years, one sure way for us to keep track of our successes (and, yes, our failures and near misses) was through the coverage we received from the media—both local and national. Every year various members of the fourth estate would descend on Vail to critique our operation and measure our progress. Sooner or later, every major league journalist who specialized in travel, food, resort architecture, or skiing showed up at Vail.

As a rule the writers were impressed with what they saw. Of course, there were shreds of criticism, too. But year after year, decade after decade, we could follow our progress by reading our press clippings. Here are a few stories in chronological order.

THE WORD GETS OUT

When our plans to develop Vail Mountain were first announced, the enthusiasm for the project was incredibly high. This story was written by Cal Queal, a longtime Denver Post *writer who followed the fortunes of Vail for many years thereafter:*

Colorado skiing took another giant jump forward Thursday with the news the state is getting still another ski area—this one the largest in the U.S. Details on the big project were first revealed in Thursday's *Denver Post*.

The Vail area, to be built on the west side of Vail Pass, sounds like a honey. It will have a large gondola lift, a pair of mile-long chair lifts, a 3,000-foot descent, wide open bowls, an alpine village—the works.

It's significant that the prime mover behind Vail is both a skier and a man who knows skiing. Pete Seibert, a well-known figure in Colorado skiing, is an expert's expert. A former FIS skier and a veteran of the famed Tenth Mountain Division, he has been associated exclusively with skiing for a long time.

With him calling the shots we can expect Vail to be a good thing.

Vail represents a personal triumph for Seibert, who has been putting the thing together since 1957. Before that, Earl Eaton had first sensed the area's potential. Listening to Seibert, we can't help but be enthusiastic about its future.

"Vail will offer runs of four miles in length on vast, open and wind-free slopes that lie entirely below timberline," Seibert said. "The combination of alpine terrain and sub-alpine weather conditions will be unique in this country."

Seibert and Eaton considered virtually every potential area in Colorado, northern New Mexico and Wyoming before making their decision. None compared to the huge snow bowls nestled against the mountains on the west side of Vail.

The gondola lift is being built by Bell Engineering, Ltd., of Lucerne, Switzerland. It will whisk skiers in enclosed comfort from the base terminal almost two miles up the mountainside in 14 minutes. The upper terminal will have an alpine restaurant designed by Fritz Benedict of Aspen, another man who does things right.

The terminal restaurant will be a fine show place for non-skiing skiers, or the jumping off place to more snow riches for the skiing skiers. They can go down or up again on a mile-long Riblet double chair. At the top of that, they can either start the long journey down or take still another run down the south slopes, served by still another double chair lift.

Sounds grand, doesn't it? Our congratulations to Pete Seibert and all the people connected with Vail. The only discordant note on the whole picture is that all this is still a year away. For us, at least, it's going to be a long wait.

From *The Denver Post*
December 29, 1961
By Cal Queal

Boom Town in a Sheep Pasture

Business writers love success stories, and in the early Sixties Vail's story was definitely a success. Willard Haselbush, business editor of The Denver Post, *wrote about us in prose that was unusually glowing for the financial page of a daily newspaper:*

Two years ago this new Colorado boomtown was a sheep pasture. Now it has $8,480,000 worth of new construction—homes, apartments, restaurants, lodges, nightclubs, shops and ski facilities—with a minimum of $3 million in construction already s et for 1964.

The growth of Vail as a year-round resort in a high valley just west of Vail Pass, 100 miles west of Denver on U.S. 6, has been so spectacular the village now has its own suburb. It's called Bighorn, three miles east of Vail Village at the foot of Vail Pass, where 129 building sites were offered for sale last March and 64 have already been sold. The sudden success of the new suburb mirrors the all but fantastic drawing power of Vail Village itself.

Construction began in Vail Village in May 1962, just 19 months ago. Since then: 50 private homes, many in the $100,000 bracket, some in the $300,000 bracket and one which cost $500,000 without landscaping and furnishings.

Among the men who own these homes hidden among the pines on the slopes of Vail Mountain are some of the big names of American industry and finance.

John Murchison, the Texas multi-millionaire who built the First National Bank skyscraper and the Denver Club

The View West of Times Square

In the frantic weeks of November 1962, while we were struggling to construct both our mountain and our village, the editors of The New York Times *sent a journalist/historian named Marshall Sprague to give their readers a view of what was going on just a few thousand miles west of Times Square:*

It has been a long time, if ever, since anyone spent $5,000,000 in a few months to start a new ski resort [Editor's Note: The number was actually half of that.]. That is the situation here, and the result is an incredible frenzy of organized chaos, scattered over six square miles of what used to be a peaceful mountain wilderness.

Today's seeming chaos at Vail is, of course, merely the appearance of modern technology applied to skiing—a far, far cry from 30 years ago when New England's pioneers started their resorts with a model-T engine and a few hundred feet of rope. Two hundred plumbers, electricians and the like reside at Vail now, mostly in trailers with many portable heated stoves, equipped with every kind of power tool. Huge transit-mix trucks climb the steep access road, mixing cement as

they head for the 200-cubic-foot anchorage of the upper gondola terminal. A tremendous crane waddled like a dinosaur up the road lately, followed by trucks from Denver loaded with concrete rafters, pre-stressed and cambered like a ski. In one day the crane lifted and placed the rafters to form the terminal's roof.

Swiss engineers in tasseled stocking caps check the lift towers, tilted perpendicular to the slope of the hill, instead of vertical, as of old. The towers came up to Vail from a Houston dock, dismantled like a toy construction set. Trucks are dumping spools of high tension wire and creosoted power poles. Linesmen, weighed down by tool vests, string wires for the 18 phones of the ski patrol.

It is hard to believe: Before Peter Seibert and Earl Eaton found Vail Mountain and named it, this whole chaotic site was a placid, oblong pile, nicely clad in aspen, spruce and lodgepole pines.

From the *New York Times*
November 18, 1962
By Marshall Sprague

building, is completing an ultra-expensive new five-level home at Vail. Next door to Murchison, a mansion has been built for Lamar Hunt, a Texas oilman who owns the Kansas City entry in the American Football League.

And what's the drawing card?

"Vail is all things to all people,"

says Gerald T. Hart, a director of Vail Associates Ltd., the development company. "It has some of the best skiing on earth—but that's only part of it."

Vail Associates Ltd. has poured $2,195,000 into skiing facilities, sewer and water system and a gas system. Another $500,000 has been budgeted for expansion of lift and mountain facilities in 1964. And now that Vail has been established as a ski center, Vail Associates, Ltd. is concentrating on developing the area into a true year-around resort.

A golf course is being laid out. Fishing facilities are being improved and new riding trails are being developed. A trapshoot installation is planned. Vail Mountain will be stocked with Himalayan blue grouse and wild turkeys for hunting on snowshoes and skis.

From *The Denver Post*
December 29, 1963
By Willard Haselbush

TIME PRAISES ANTELOPE SCHNITZEL BUT DUMPS SEIBERT FROM COVER

In December 1972, TIME magazine published a cover story that focused on the boom in skiing. TIME chose Vail as the centerpiece resort for the whole world, and I nearly got my lovely puss portrayed on the cover of 4,000,000 magazines. At the last minute, the editors of TIME decided to go with a pretty woman from Seattle. I didn't mind as much as I might have because the story turned out to be basically another love gusher of the kind we were used to. But it wasn't all positive and it put a spotlight on what Vail had come to be after being in business for 10 years.

The Ted Kennedys, the John Lindsays and the Charles Percys ski there. After a hard day on the slopes, the nightlife warms up in the 30 restaurants and bars, and skiers cluster over Swiss wine and antelope schnitzel at Gashof Gramshammer, which is owned by Pepi, the famed Austrian ski champion. The younger set is likely to converge at Donovan's Copper Bar and the Nu

EAST COAST SOPHISTICATE DISCOVERS VAIL

In 1964, Sport Illustrated's cosmopolitan ski editor, Fred R. Smith, weighed in with a hugely enthusiastic progress report that managed not to mention grouse, golf, mushrooms, or baton twirlers:

It is difficult to believe, but three winters ago there was no Vail. Truckers or skiers bound for Aspen coasting west from the 12,000-foot heights of Colorado's Loveland Pass and the Continental Divide might have paused to admire this tree-lined trout stream, a herd of mule deer or even a Rocky Mountain bighorn ram, silhouetted on a rim of red rock. They would have seen little else.

Today in the vicinity of Gore Creek, where not even a mining shack existed before, a dozen saunas now flourish. Steam rises from three outdoor, heated swimming pools, and smoke escapes the chimneys of 72 houses, ranging from a ski chateau with walls painted in trompe l'oeil to simply rustic cottages furnished with relics of Colorado silver-mining camps. A liquor store is stocked with western-size bottles of Beefeater and with Pommard and Muscadets that would do a Madison Avenue vintner proud. Blanquette de veau is served in a downstairs boîte called La Cave where Colorado University students in jeans dance a Wild West version of the Watusi and Long Island ladies in long skirts do genteel versions of the frug.

The chalets, the saunas, the Pommard and the frug are the appurtenances of ski areas around the world. But never in the history of U.S. skiing have they all come so quickly, never has a bare mountain leaped in such a short time into the four-star category of ski resorts...

(Today) Vail represents a total commitment of $15 million, with a sizable share of that investment in some of the most interesting ski houses in America...

Vail can now sleep from 1,200 to 1,500 transient skiers in rental houses and apartments, a 106-unit motel and six inns and pensions. From the beginning, Vail has been a family sort of area, with most people entertaining at home. The boy-meets-girl set has found Vail pale at night, particularly by Aspen standards....

All of the apparently disparate building of bars and houses, apartments and shops could well have turned the village into an architectural abomination. It did not. Vail is a model ski town. The resort's planning board, with resident architect Fitzhugh Scott in charge, has achieved a harmonious balance. No cars are allowed—or needed—in the village center, which has the pleasing aspect of a Tyrolean village set in the spacious American West.

Although Vail has acquired a reputation for being an "in" place to ski, no chichi or jet-set snobbery has developed. The people you meet on the mountain who ask you to come by for a sauna or tea may have spent a mint on their chalet—or they may have built it themselves.

From *Sports Illustrated*
November 23, 1964
By Fred R. Smith

Gnu or the Ore House where the talk seems to focus on skiing above all else —even sex. The newest favorite place is the Ichiban, a Japanese restaurant run by a dental hygienist, an architect and a sociologist—all under 30—who left careers in Boston and Seattle in order to live close to the mountain. This is the scene at Vail, Colorado, an instant alpine community that is the most successful winter resort built in the U.S. in the last decade.

As in any ski town there are problems of extreme expansion and contraction. The population swells from 700 in the summer to 10,000 in the winter. On weekends, Vail's eight policemen, normally preoccupied with nothing more serious than ski equipment thefts (the biggest crime category), struggle with monumental parking jams. There is also a shortage of moderate-income housing for Vail's ski instructors, waiters and salespeople, many of whom live in a trailer camp a dozen miles away. The town manager, Terrell Minger, 30, cannot afford to buy a place in Vail on his $21,000 salary.

The permanent year-round residents who hired Minger and run the town are mostly conservative, family-oriented folk. They can afford to pay $35,000 or more for condominiums. Houses on the golf course area start at $90,000, and Texas Oilman John Murchison's glass-and-aspen vacation house is probably worth $500,000. For years, anyone thought to be a hippie was not overly welcome, and longhairs found it difficult to get work or a pad. Youthful counterculturists discovered that Vail was not the best place to be a ski bum, particularly after local police

pulled some tough drug busts. When Minger showed up for the job wearing a mustache four years ago, some locals told him that he was unacceptable. Only lately has Vail Associates, which runs the ski area, dropped its rule that bearded residents could not get special-rate local lift tickets.

The town's great problem has been gaining a sense of identity. Says Minger: "We are a teenager as a community. Vail started out as sort of a country club and became a company town. Now we are finally moving toward something that resembles a community. We are no longer just a product, and we are not plastic either. Real people live here..."

What the community needs most, he suggests, is something beyond skiing and summer leisure, perhaps an "industry of the mind" or a center for the performing arts...

When Vail Associates grew so big that it could no longer be run by Pete Seibert alone, he moved up from president to chairman. As the new president, the company recruited Richard L. Peterson, a Harvard M.B.A. The two men also brought in several other business school grads, giving Vail professional management. Last year the company grossed $6,700,000 from lifts, ski school, restaurants and land sales, and earned $812,100 after taxes. Expanding, it recently spent $4,600,000 for 2,200 acres at Beaver Creek, seven miles from the main development: the area is scheduled to open in 1975.

Seibert himself owns Vail stock worth more than $600,000. But, he insists: "Money is really not my thing.

More important, I'm right where I have wanted to be since I was a kid. Driving at night sometimes, I come round that turn at the end of the valley—and suddenly I see the lights. Then it comes back to me that there was nothing here, nothing at all, not very long ago."

From *TIME*
December 25, 1972

THE FUN IN VAIL

SKIING Magazine's John Jerome was impressed when he returned to Vail "City" in 1975, after a two-year hiatus from the mountain.

Vail invented fun skiing.

Now, there are plenty of other places where it is fun to ski, of course, and some of them will dispute Vail's claim to the invention. But it's a fact. Vail invented the idea of providing a whole mountainful of perfect, broad, open-slope, moderately challenging skiing. The kind of skiing where your speed depends almost entirely on your courage, where you tend to build up a head of steam and just cruise, throwing great, sweeping turns, tears from the wind streaming down your cheeks, skis rippling underfoot, snow like silk. Skiing the shape of the slope, which is the shape of the mountain itself, rather than the shape of the hack-work done by the several thousand skiers who have preceded you.

There is indeed a whole mountainful of just that kind of skiing awaiting you at Vail. (That doesn't mean that there is no other kind of skiing at Vail, but first things first in this narrative.) It is so distinctive a category of skiing that it should perhaps be designated

"Vail-type" skiing. But the interesting thing is that in its 13 years of operation, Vail has now fed so many people into the sport—so many who have carried Vail's vision on into the wider world of skiing, so many from the Midwest and the East—that we've come to identify Vail's product with the entire West. What is really (or originally) Vail-type skiing has become a generic concept: Western skiing. The broad slopes and big cruising and big cruising turns, yes, but also sparkling sun and snow that goes on forever and the crisp bit of high-altitude air and all the rest. Western American skiing. The best there is, the best in the world.

All Vail has done is take that fairly simple notion—fun skiing—and with it build one of the most successful ski resorts in the world. Vail...works. Let me tell you of my innocence: I manage to get back to Vail every other year or so, and although it always seems to double in size between those visits, I was not—couldn't have been—prepared for last year. I'd missed a couple of years at Vail, which by chance were the Gerald Ford years, although that was certainly not the only force at work to keep Vail changing. When I came driving into the Gore Creek Valley last winter, arriving unaccustomedly from the west, I simply could not believe my eyes. Couldn't believe Vail. When I'd last seen it, Vail was already a very large resort, consisting of Vail Village plus some rather frantic construction activity at Lionshead, where the Gondola II already reached up the mountain. Now, it was...a city. There is no other term for it.

The space between "old" Vail Village and Lionshead is now completely filled with buildings—most of them high-rise condominiums. Vail has a telephone building, a municipal building, a Public Service Co. building. A four-story, $4 million transportation center. It has a bank, print shops, furniture stores. There are, in residence, an optometrist, an ophthalmologist, and two dentists. Eight construction firms; three advertising agencies! Vail has street numbers now. You have to look up addresses in the directory. A ski resort with street numbers: Fit that into your notions of the sport, ski tourers.

More naïveté: I thought I had my reservations in order, to spend a few days in Vail after Washington's Birthday week was over. I had goofed—my error entirely—and a few days before my arrival, when I tried to confirm, I found myself out of luck. Because I was on assignment, I leaned on Vail's able press people for help. They got me in, barely, in a condominium ($56 a night, no credit cards accepted) that does not even appear on the map of Vail. Vail was literally full. With beds for 15,000, Vail was running at capacity, as it had the week before, as it would every week through the remainder of the season. Running at capacity despite a still-floundering economy and the worst Rocky Mountain snow conditions in history.

That is how well Vail works. It is full—and very few other ski resorts in the world can make that statement. When Vail is full, it has 62 restaurants full, more than 30 heated swimming pools full, 20—count 'em, 20—ski shops full. Any ski resort operating at capacity must necessarily have lift lines, and Vail had them when I was there—

although with a lift capacity of nearly 19,000 skiers per hour, the waits are seldom terribly burdensome. The Vail level of capacity also means restaurant-line waits, ski-shop–line waits. The perfectly shocking truth about Vail is that with all those big numbers—the 62 restaurants and 20 ski shops and all the rest—more is needed. Vail is crowded, with all that capacity. That's how well Vail works. That's how well Fun Skiing works.

What Vail has done, brilliantly, is present skiing as, basically, a non-sweaty sport. Vail was built with sweat, is run with sweat, but run so that the customers don't have to see the sweaty part. Its straight-arrow hiring practices and concern with control have offended some of skiing's freer spirits, but it must be remembered that Vail is skiing's only successful New Town. Everyone who has started a ski resort in the past 30 years has always talked about building a whole new town around the skiing facility, but Vail is the only one that pulled it off.

You might want to go see Vail on that score alone, simply to observe the phenomenon. But don't get too obsessed with sociological observation or you may overlook the other basic truth about Vail, which is those miles and miles of sheer skiing up there, just waiting for you. That's the part that knocked me on my preconceived notions. Vail was as enjoyable last winter, in wall-to-wall people, as it had been in 1965—with half the crowds and one-third the facilities. Different, God knows, but as enjoyable. Half familiar, half delightfully new. Riva Ridge and Prima, as familiar now as old

Vail Associates Lets George Do It

In July 1985 Vail became part of George Gillett's vast business empire:

For the second time in a month, a buyer has stepped forward with a multimillion dollar bid for controlling interest in Vail Associates.

The latest purchaser, Gillett Group—an entertainment and communications holding company of Geroge N. Gillett, a one-time owner of the Harlem Globetrotters—will pay $55 million.

In a two-step deal, Gillett has agreed to buy the 42 percent common share interest of Goliad Oil and Gas Trust, a holding of the Texas Bass brothers, for $35 a share. That's only 12.5 cents more than last month's carbon copy deal which fell through July 9.

Gillett will also pay $2.5 million for the 500,000 preferred shares. The final step will be to offer $35 for all the remaining common stock.

The deal is expected to close in 60 days. "This time there aren't any major hurdles," said Harry H. Frampton III, president of Vail Associates, which operates the ski resorts of Vail and Beaver Creek.

On June 22, Vail Associates announced that Denver developers Bill L. Walters, Nick Hackstock and European Ferries Inc., owner of the Denver Technological Center, had agreed to buy the Goliad interest—at $34.875 a share and the 500,000 shares of preferred stock for $2.5 million—a $26.9 million deal.

On July 9, the deal was called off; the only explanation given was that the action was taken "by mutual consent."

In 1982 *Fortune* magazine ranked the Nashville-based Gillett Group among the top 50 private industrial companies, estimating its annual sales at $430 million.

Gillett was president and chief executive of Globe communications—which owned the Harlem Globetrotters—from 1967 to 1977 when he organized the Gillett Group. Prior to that he was business manager of the Miami Dolphins after a stint as a management consultant with McKinsey & Co, a management consulting firm based in California...

"We have a great sense of appreciation for the Vail Valley," Gillett said in the statement. "We are committed to the Vail Mountain improvement program and the continued quality development of Beaver Creek."

Gillett and his family own a home in Vail.

From *The Denver Post*
July 23, 1985
By Gail L. Pitts

ski boots—and still challenging. The whistling expanses of the back bowls. All that new stuff in the Northeast Bowl. Mountain, everywhere I looked, just waiting to be skied. The hassles were worth it. It is reassuring, somehow, to find that in one of the most successful ski resorts in the world, the skiing is still so good. I don't know what else I was expecting—that Vail had forgotten how they did it? That all those people could somehow have worn the mountain out? They haven't. It's still there, and there is now more of it.

And all the rest of you skiers, well, we'll see you there eventually. Vail is the Times Square of skiing: Spend enough time there, wandering around the village or up skiing the mountain, and you are bound to run into everyone you've ever known in skiing. I guarantee it.

From SKIING Magazine
November 1976
By John Jerome

Finally, Beaver Creek is Born

There wasn't much snow, but there was plenty of enthusiasm when Beaver Creek opened in December of 1980, even from people like Colorado's governor, who had bitterly opposed it:

Jean-Claude Killy just happened to drop by. So did former President Gerald Ford and enough other dignitaries to make it one of the most impressive gatherings since they started making mountains.

Ten years and $40 million later, they opened Beaver Creek resort Sunday to the crisp sound of champagne corks popping and the muffled noise of heavy

A Lifetime of Parking

The people who bought the lifetime parking spaces probably weren't the same people who complained about lift ticket prices:

When Vail Associates put underground parking spaces on sale for $30,000, some of the locals chuckled.

They aren't chuckling anymore. Most of those spaces have been sold, a year before the garage opens, and the price has climbed to $45,000, plus an annual payment of $1,350.

"We'll keep raising (the price) incrementally as we feel the market will bear," said Dave Corbin, vice president of development for Vail Associates Real Estate Group.

The spaces will be in an underground garage dubbed the Golden Peak Passport Club, scheduled to open next season at the east base of the ski area. Fifty of 75 so-called Tier I spaces have been sold.

In addition to the up-front money, Tier I parking space owners—they're called "members"—will pay annual dues of $1,350. The money will go toward Passport Club programs, maintenance and labor costs, said Joe Malone, project director for Vail Associates Real Estate Group.

Club members will be greeted by a ski valet and will have use of lockers, ski storage and boot dryers. The club will offer private reception and dining areas.

Three well-heeled skiers so far are paying for both the Passport Club parking spaces and a membership in the separate Game Creek Club, a private dining facility on Vail Mountain. It is set to open Feb. 1.

Founding members of Game Creek are paying $75,000 each plus annual dues of $1,200. The club will offer an upscale European-style restaurant plus concierge service and a business communications center.

Vail Associates is talking to other Game Creek members about buying parking spaces. "We've had a fairly good response from them," Malone said.

After 30 years, the ski company will return initiation fees, without interest, to Passport Club members.

Owners may also sell their parking spaces.

The parking structure is part of a $27 million redevelopment of the ski mountain's eastern ski base.

From *The Denver Post*
January 11, 1996
By Allison Anderson

An Icon Falls

In the ultimate panty raid, hooligans cut down Vail's most famous tree in April 1997:

The notorious Panty Tree above Vail's Chair 5 base area was chopped down Saturday night by vandals who apparently hiked into the resort's back bowls with a bow saw.

The infamous aspen, for years a chronicler of the steamier side of the area's local mountain life, was felled without Vail Associates or U.S. Forest Service permission, along with several surrounding trees that had caught stray lingerie thrown from the lift, officials said.

"It was not any of our staff people," Vail Associates spokesman Rob Perlman said. "This was done by an unknown person or persons. (Vail) ski patrol did report it to the U.S. Forest Service as they would any malicious act against Forest Service property."

In all, five trees were cut down, Perlman said. "They cut down and left the trees with the underwear still in them," he said. Placed in nearby tree as a symbol of goodwill to the local tradition, undergarments recovered from the felled aspen were redeposited into a nearby tree.

"We made an attempt to try and place the miscellaneous items in proximity of the original Panty Tree," Perlman said, adding that there were no suspects.

"The panty perp is still at large," he said.

"We're actually trying to speculate (on the culprit) ourselves. We thought maybe it was someone who didn't want their panties to be in that tree.

"It is our official position that this is

not related to the Hale-Bopp [comet]."

Perlman said whoever cut down the trees Saturday night went to a lot of trouble.

"My guess would be they rode up the gondola and snowshoed or walked from there," he said.

That scenario would have meant a ridgeline traverse to the top of chair 5 at 11,250 feet, a 1,650-foot descent to the Panty Tree and climb back up, and another 2,000-foot descent to Vail Village.

"We're talking miles," Perlman said.

Forest Service officials speculated the culprit may have stayed on the mountain after the lifts closed, hiked out of the back bowls and skied down.

"There are definitely fines involved with cutting any type of green timber without a permit," said Bruce Ungari, winter sports administrator for the Holy Cross Ranger District.

"It's pretty unusual circumstances. We definitely do not condone it. It's a violation of federal regulations."

If someone is found responsible for the incident, the Forest Service will issue citations of $75 per tree, Ungari said, and the matter could go to federal court, where a fine of up to $5,000 could be imposed.

Last ski season, efforts to start a version of Vail's Panty Tree at the more family-oriented Beaver Creek ski area, also owned by Vail Associates, were thwarted when company officials cut down a bra- and panty-sprouting aspen midway up the Centennial Express lift.

From *The Denver Post*
April 1, 1997
By Dan Sullivan

BLUE SKY BASIN OPENS

In the winter of 2000 came the final piece of the puzzle Earl Eaton and I had started 43 years before:

It's not often that 6,000 skiers and snowboarders are waiting in line for a single chairlift. But a scene reminiscent of a 19th century land rush occurred here early last month when Vail cut the ribbon on the vast backcountry of its controversial Blue Sky Basin.

"I was down at the chairlift when the first surge from the top came down," said Kelly Ladyga, a spokeswoman for adjoing Beaver Creek. "All of a sudden, 300 snowboarders came shooting through the trees. It looked like we were being attacked. I thought, 'Oh, my God!'"

Vail's management committed five years and $20 million in development costs, and took intense heat—literally—from environmentalists to make Blue Sky happen. On October 19, 1998, a predawn fire incinerated three of Vail's mountaintop buildings and damaged four chairlifts. An organization called the Earth Liberation Front claimed responsibility for setting the fire in protest over Blue Sky Basin. Although no one was injured in the blaze, the ecoterrorist attack cost Vail $12 million and much of its sense of well-being.

Efforts to bring Blue Sky Basin into Vail's 5,100-acre fold continued despite the trouble. It was developed with permission of the Forest Service, which leases the land to Vail. But for environmentalists, Blue Sky meant the loss of yet another wild expanse.

"It's better than I even thought it was going to be," Bill Jensen, Vail's chief operating officer, said in an interview here. "I remember standing on a ridge at Blue Sky three years ago as it was evolving. The company wanted then to make it unique, to make it different than the rest of Vail, and that's what it is."

It is all of that. Gliding down the face of Pete's Bowl, one of the area's two wide basins, takes a visitor on a brush with nature not found at most modern mountain resorts. Stands of aspen trees, fir and pine become roundabouts for skiers on a downhill cruise; boulders and cliff precipices become magnets for snowboarders on a joy ride.

The partly groomed area is mostly for intermediate and expert levels and it takes a certain panache to ski or ride it well. Trails as such do not exist. Instead, skiers and boarders thread their way down from the 11,480-foot summit like hikers on a winding footpath.

In keeping with its natural landscape, Blue Sky Basin has new buildings with a rustic look. The area's only lodge so far is a warming hut. Rough-hewn log furniture is arranged around a fireplace, albeit gas burning with fake logs. No food is for sale; there isn't even a soda machine.

Made of cement and stone, the hut has a concrete exterior made to look like wood. An adjacent shed for the chairlift summit is made of faux wood, designed to look like a barn. But Jensen concedes that a restaurant is probably in the future.

Despite Blue Sky's concessions to nature, adversaries are still rankled. Jeff Berman, president of Colorado Wild, an environmental group that is opposed to the development of Blue Sky Basin, is concerned about the precedent it sets.

Colorado Wild opposed the expansion on several levels, one of which was development of a ski area in lynx habitat. Vail has insisted that none of the feline species, which is on the endangered list, have been seen in the Blue Sky area since early in the 1970s. Berman disagrees, noting that biologists have documented lynx tracks there.

Jenson answers the critics with a question. "When is enough enough in the mountains?" he said. "Ten or 15 years ago, environmentalists said there should be no new ski areas. Now the battle cry is that they're opposed to any ski area expansion. Society changes, and there are environmental pressures. But I absolutely believe there has to be a balance between biodiversity and expansion."

Since the fires, the 25,000-foot Two Elk lodge adjacent to Blue Sky that burned has been rebuilt. Its $10.3 million replacement duplicates the previous lodge in almost every respect—the same carpeting, log pillars and American Indian paintings.

Made of real wood, the new lodge is surrounded by an outdoor fire sprinkling system as well as one indoors. Video cameras scan its perimeters day and night, and a new addition houses apartments for four Vail employees to watch over them.

From *the New York Times*
February 10, 2000
By Barbara Lloyd **V**

A SLIPPERY PRINCESS

In 1994 Vail proved a tough place for the paparazzi to track down Princess Di:

Rumors were piling up deeper than fresh powder on Vail Mountain yesterday as Princess Diana continued to dodge journalists during her third day of skiing here.

The Princess of Wales skied on seven inches of new snow with a small group of friends, while a large cadre of international photographers and journalists unsuccessfully tailed her.

"It's like a feeding frenzy out there," said Paul Witt, spokesman for Vail Associates Inc., owner of Vail, Beaver Creek and Arrowhead ski areas. More than 100 press inquiries have been logged at Vail Associates offices since news broke that Diana began a ski holiday here Wednesday.

Reporters still haven't confirmed where the elusive princess is staying, but locals remain nonplussed by the royal visit.

"Everyone was really mellow. People weren't bothering her," said local skier Chris Anthony, who spotted Princess Di in a chairlift line. "People definitely knew who she was, but they just looked at her."

Photographers crowded around chairlifts in Vail Village yesterday morning, hoping to snap a photo that could be worth as much as $50,000 to the London tabloids.

Diana reportedly told Vail Associates officials that she won't pose for an official publicity shot, something she typically did before she split from Prince Charles and the royal family.

Tabloid journalists also were following ski instructors around town, staking out homes where the royal skier is thought to be visiting and hanging out in trendy restaurants.

Witt said he has never seen a stronger press reaction since he has worked at the company.

"This is bigger than when Clinton came here," he said, referring to the President's 1993 summer golfing trip to Vail.

Diana has kept a low profile during her Vail visit, but she has been spotted around town.

She ate lunch and dinner in Vail Village on Wednesday and has been spotted skiing groomed runs with ski instructor Pentti Tofferi on Vail Mountain all week.

She was seen working out for an hour Thursday night on a treadmill at the Cascade Club, wearing a black warmup sweater and white tights.

"She was stunning, gorgeous," said a local who didn't want his name printed. "No one bothered her. They left her alone, but people obviously noticed her."

She ate lunch at a private cabin Thursday with a small group of friends, including Rod Slifer, a local real estate developer who reportedly rented her the home where she is staying.

Just where she is staying remains unconfirmed. Several British tabloids reported she is at the home of millionaire Los Angeles publisher Michael Flannery in the exclusive Forest Road neighborhood at the base of Vail Mountain.

A call to the house yesterday resulted in a hangup. Photographers staked out the house, but no one spotted any evidence of Diana.

The ski-in, ski-out, $4.1 million house is in the same ritzy neighborhood where Texas billionaire Ross Perot and New York financier Henry Kravis own homes.

The hunt to spot Di grows frenzied but proves fruitless

From *The Denver Post*
December 31, 1994
By Andrew Hood

ACKNOWLEDGEMENTS

I am indebted to the following people who helped me build the dream, live the dream, and tell the story of the dream:

First and foremost, I'd like to dedicate this book to Earl Eaton, who discovered Vail Mountain and recognized its remarkable potential as a vast, rolling playground for winter sports. Earl is a true mountain man and a great friend.

Secondly, my deepest thanks to those pioneers who shared my dream of a great mountain resort in the Colorado Rockies and struggled to make it happen. These citizens of Vail came from all over the world—men and women who were looking for new challenges and a new way of life. Some of them planned on staying only a year or two—and ended up making Vail their home. Their belief in the idea of Vail, and their determination to make it happen, was truly inspiring.

Thirdly, I'd like to thank the following people who helped me write the Vail story and find the pictures to illustrate it. For their input and their time I am grateful.

Jack Affleck	Christy Hill
Adam Aron	Bill Johnson
Apollo Ski Partners	Jean-Claude Killy
Aspen Historical Society	Jim Mandel
Bill Brown	Mark Manley
George Caulkins	Chupa Nelson
Cindy Clement	Bob Parker
Colorado Ski Museum staff	Irv Post
Andy Daly	Cal Queal
Denver Public Library, Western History Section staff	Marc Rowan
Sigi Faller	Morrie Shepard
Dave and Renee Gorsuch	Rod Slifer
Pepi and Sheika Gramshammer	June Simonton
Harley Higbie	Tenth Mountain Division Association
Paul Hauk	Paul Testwuide
Marty Head	Vail Resorts

My special thanks to my assistant, Kelly Davis, who chased down information, collected photos, and basically kept me on track through this long process.

Finally, my sincere thanks to my editors and friends at Mountain Sports Press, a division of Times Mirror Magazines: Mark Doolittle; Ian Ferguson; Bill Grout; Dan Kasper; and Michelle Klammer.

Without the support of my family, Vail would not have been built and this book would not have been written. Left: the Seibert family at Mid Vail in 1962-63. Front row, left to right: Calvin, Brant, and Peter Jr.; back row: Betty and Pete.

COVER ....Dan Coffey

p. 1 ....David Lokey
p. 2 ....Vail Resorts
p. 7 ....Skiing Magazine Archive

PHOTO GALLERY
pp. 10-25 ....Vail Resorts

CHAPTER 1
pp. 26, 27 ....Vail Resorts
p. 28 ....Peter Seibert Collection
p. 29 ....Vail Resorts
p. 30 (top) ....The Denver Public Library, Western History Collection
p. 30 (bottom) ....Peter Seibert Collection
p. 31 (top) ....Peter Runyan/Vail Resorts
p. 31 (bottom) ....Vail Resorts
p. 32 ....Peter Runyan/Vail Resorts
p. 33 ....The Denver Public Library, Western History Collection

CHAPTER 2
p. 34 ....Kaia von Praag/Vail Resorts
pp. 36, 37 ....Vail Resorts
p. 38 ....Jack Affleck/Vail Resorts
p. 39, 40 ....Vail Resorts
p. 41 ....Jack Affleck/Vail Resorts

CHAPTER 3
p. 42 ....Mark Doolittle
pp. 44, 45 ....Peter Seibert Collection
p. 46 ....Vail Resorts
pp. 47, 48 ....Peter Seibert Collection
p. 49 ....Lu Stubbs

CHAPTER 4
p. 50 ....The Denver Public Library, Western History Collection
pp. 52, 53 ....Peter Seibert Collection
pp. 54, 55 ....The Denver Public Library, Western History Collection
p. 56 ....Courtesy, Aspen Historical Society
p. 57 ....The Denver Public Library, Western History Collection
p. 58 ....Peter Seibert Collection
pp. 59, 61 ....The Denver Public Library, Western History Collection

CHAPTER 5
pp. 62, 64 ....Courtesy, Aspen Historical Society
pp. 65, 66, 67 ....Peter Seibert Collection
pp. 68, 69 ....Courtesy, Aspen Historical Society
p. 70 ....Skiing Magazine Archive
p. 71 (top) ....Peter Seibert Collection
p. 71 (bottom) ....Courtesy, Aspen Historical Society

CHAPTER 6
p. 72 ....Colin Samuels
p. 74 ....Peter Seibert Collection
p. 75 ....SKI Magazine
p. 76 ....Peter Seibert Collection
p. 77 ....Colin Samuels
pp. 78, 79 ....Peter Seibert Collection
p. 80 ....James Bracken/Silverton Chamber of Commerce
p. 81 ....Peter Seibert Collection

CHAPTER 7
p. 82 ....Hal Shelton/Peter Seibert Collection

pp. 84, 85 ....Vail Resorts
pp. 86, 88 ....The Denver Public Library, Western History Collection
pp. 89, 90 ....Vail Resorts
p. 91 ....Peter Seibert Collection
pp. 92, 93 ....Vail Resorts

CHAPTER 8
p. 94, ...Vail Resorts
p. 96 ....The Denver Public Library, Western History Collection
pp. 97, 98, 99, ...Vail Resorts
p. 101 ....The Denver Public Library, Western History Collection

CHAPTER 9
p. 102 ....D. Conger
p. 104 (top) ....The Denver Public Library, Western History Collection
p. 104 (bottom) ....Vail Resorts
p. 105, 107 ....The Denver Public Library, Western History Collection

CHAPTER 10
p. 108 ....Peter Runyan/Vail Resorts
p. 110 ....Vail Resorts
p. 111 ....Peter Runyon/Vail Resorts
p. 112 (top) ....Vail Resorts
p. 112 (bottom) ....Peter Runyon/Vail Resorts
p. 113 (top) ....D. Conger
pp. 113 (bottom), 114 ...Vail Resorts
p. 115 ....Peter Runyan/Vail Resorts
p. 116 (top) ....Vail Resorts
p. 116 (bottom) ....Bruce Barthel
pp. 118, 119 ....Peter Runyon/Vail Resorts
p. 120 (top) ....Vail Resorts
p. 120 (bottom) ....Peter Runyon/Vail Resorts
pp. 121, 122, 123 ......Vail Resorts

CHAPTER 11
pp. 124, 126 ....Peter Runyon/Vail Resorts
p. 127 ....Vail Resorts
pp. 129, 131, 132 ......Peter Runyon/Vail Resorts
p. 133 ....Barry Stott/Vail Resorts

CHAPTER 12
pp. 134, 136-139 ....Vail Resorts
p. 140 (top) ....Jack Affleck/Vail Resorts
pp. 140 (bottom), 141 ...Vail Resorts

CHAPTER 13
p. 142 ....Duane Nelson
pp. 144, 147, 149-153 ....Vail Resorts

COLOR GALLERY
p. 154 ....D. Conger
p. 156 ....Dan Coffey
pp. 158, 159 ....Vail Resorts
p. 160 ....Peter Runyon/Vail Resorts
p. 162 ....Tom Rushkind
p. 163 ....Ken Redding
p. 164 ....Dan Coffey
p. 166 ....Vail Resorts
pp. 167, 168 ....Jack Affleck/Vail Resorts
p. 170 ....Frank Wilcox
pp. 171 ....Peter Runyon/Vail Resorts
pp. 172-175 ....Vail Resorts
p. 176, 177 ....Dan Coffey